Help Me! Guide to the iPhone 5S

By Charles Hughes

Table of Contents

Getting Started

Table of Contents

1. Button Layout

The iPhone has four buttons and one switch. The rest of the functionality is controlled by the touchscreen. Each button has several functions, depending on the context in which it is used. The iPhone buttons perform the following functions:

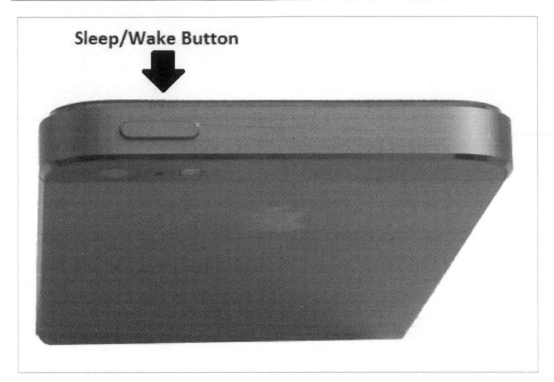

Figure 1: Top View

Sleep/Wake Button

- Turns the iPhone on and off.
- Locks and unlocks the iPhone.

Home Button

Figure 2: Front View

Home Button

- Shows the Home screen.
- Displays open applications when pressed twice quickly.

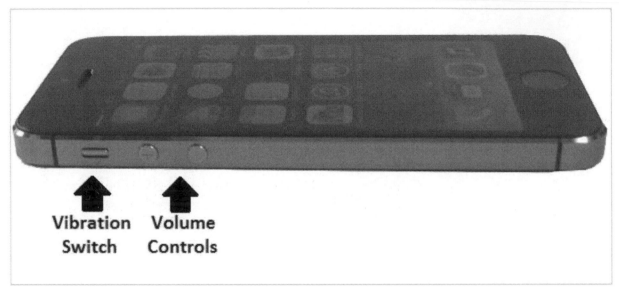

Figure 3: Side View

Volume Controls

- Control the volume of the ringer. Refer to *"Adjusting the Settings"* on page 208 to learn more about setting ringtones or the sound volume.
- Control the volume of the earpiece or speakerphone during a conversation.
- Control the media volume.

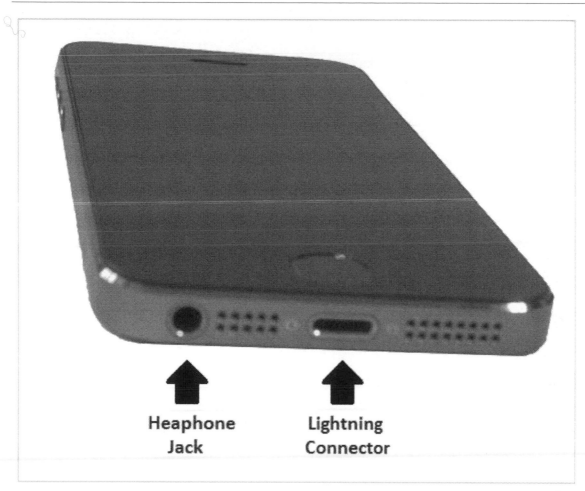

Figure 4: Bottom View

Headphone Jack - Allows headphones or speakers to be plugged in. Allows an AUX cable to be plugged in to hear the iPhone over the speakers in a car or stereo.

Lightning Connector - Connects the iPhone to a computer in order to transfer data. Connects the iPhone to a charger.

2. Charging the iPhone

To ensure that the iPhone works well, please follow these guidelines:
Note: You cannot use a cable that came with any earlier generation iPhone to charge the iPhone 5S.

Discharge the iPhone completely at least once a month. When charging the battery, the meter in the upper right-hand corner of the screen (when unlocked) may show that it is fully charged; however, the charge is not complete until **100% Charged** appears on the lock screen. Insert the Lightning cable into the Lightning Connector on the bottom of the phone. When the cable is inserted correctly, the indicator sound is played or the iPhone vibrates. Refer to *"Tips and Tricks"* on page 294 to learn about conserving battery life.

3. Turning the iPhone On and Off

Use the Sleep/Wake button to turn the iPhone on or off. To turn the iPhone on, press and hold

the **Sleep/Wake** button for two seconds. The iPhone turns on and the logo is displayed. After the iPhone has finished starting up, the Lock screen is displayed.
Note: If the iPhone does not turn on after a few seconds, try charging the battery.
To turn the iPhone off, press and hold the **Sleep/Wake** button until the screen becomes dark. The

message "Slide to power off" appears. Touch the slider and move your finger to the right. The iPhone turns off.
Note: To keep the iPhone on, press "Cancel" or do not take any action at all.

4. Installing a SIM Card

Insert the SIM card from an old phone to retain your personal information and phone number. The iPhone 5S only takes nano SIM cards. The type of SIM card also depends on your carrier. For instance, you cannot insert a Verizon SIM card into an AT&T iPhone, and vice-versa. To install a SIM card:

1. Insert the end of a paper clip or a SIM eject tool into the hole on the right side of the iPhone. The SIM card tray pops out.
2. Take out the old SIM card, if necessary, and insert the new SIM card with the short side facing upwards.
3. Re-insert the tray into the iPhone. The new SIM card is installed.

5. Setting Up the iPhone for the First Time

You must set up the iPhone 5S when you turn it on for the first time. To set up the iPhone 5S:

1. Turn on the iPhone by pressing and holding the **Power** button until the icon appears. The iPhone starts up and the Welcome screen appears, as shown in **Figure 5**.
2. Touch the screen anywhere and move your finger to the right to begin setting up your iPhone. The Language screen appears, as shown in **Figure 6**.
3. Touch the preferred language. The language is selected and the Country screen appears, as shown in **Figure 7**.
4. Touch the country in which you reside. The Wi-Fi Networks screen appears.
5. Touch a Wi-Fi network. The Password prompt appears.
6. Enter the network password, usually found on your wireless router. Touch Join in the upper right-hand corner of the screen. The iPhone connects to the selected Wi-Fi network and the Location Services screen appears, as shown in **Figure 8**.
7. Touch Enable Location Services if you want to turn the feature on. Touch Disable Location Services to leave the feature turned off. Some applications will not work with Location Services turned off. The Set Up iPhone screen appears, as shown in **Figure 9**.
8. Touch Restore from iCloud Backup or Restore from iTunes Backup if you have a data backup. You will need to connect the iPhone to your computer and run iTunes if you touch 'Restore from iTunes Backup'. Touch Set Up as New iPhone if you do not have an iCloud or iTunes backup. The Apple ID screen appears.
9. Touch Sign In with your Apple ID if you have an Apple ID or touch Create a Free Apple ID. The Terms and Conditions screen appears once you are signed in.
10. Touch Agree in the bottom right-hand corner of the screen. A confirmation dialog appears.
11. Touch Agree again. The iCloud screen appears, as shown in **Figure 10**.
12. Touch **Use iCloud** to use the feature or touch **Don't Use iCloud** to disable it. The iCloud Backup screen appears if you touched 'Use iCloud'. The Find My iPhone screen appears. \
13. Touch **Use Find My iPhone** to use the feature or **Don't Use Find My iPhone** to disable it. 'Find My iPhone' is a free service. The iMessage and FaceTime screen appears.
14. Touch a phone number or email address if you would like to enable it for iMessage or FaceTime. A blue check mark appears next to each selected address or number. Touch **Next** in the upper right-hand corner of the screen when you are finished.
15. The Passcode Creation screen appears, as shown in **Figure 11**. Enter a passcode to set up a security lock for your phone, or touch **Don't Add Passcode** to do it later. The Diagnostics screen appears.
16. Touch **Automatically Send** to have the iPhone send usage data to Apple or touch **Don't Send** to disable this feature. Usage Data contains anonymous statistics about the ways in which you use your iPhone.
17. Touch **Get Started**. The iPhone setup is complete.

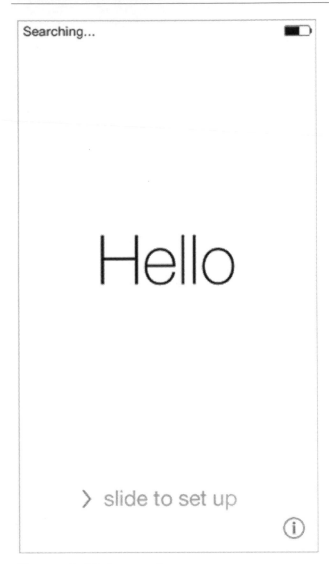

Figure 5: Welcome Screen

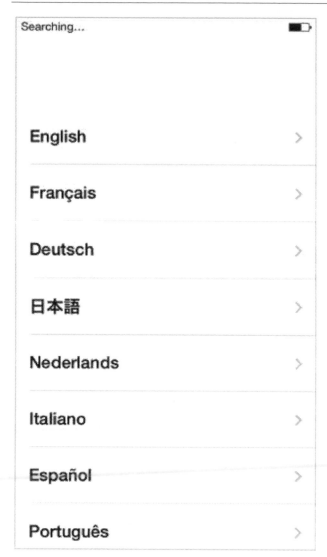

Figure 6: Language Screen

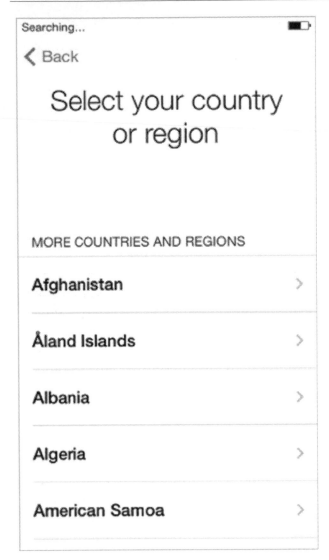

Figure 7: Country Screen

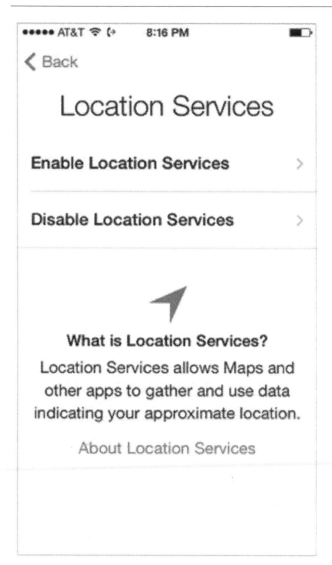

Figure 8: Location Services Screen

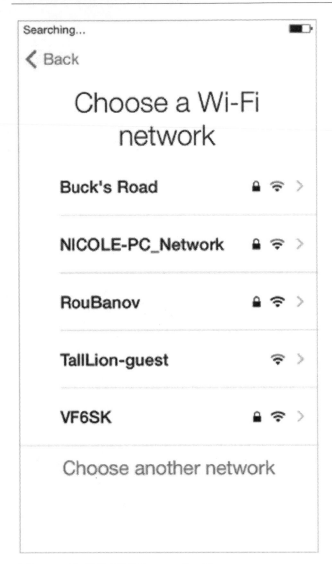

Figure 9: Wi-Fi Networks Screen

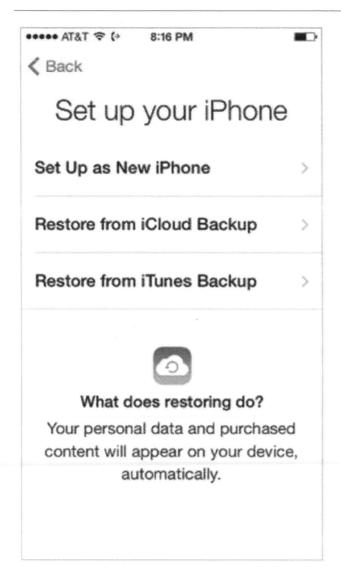

Figure 10: Set Up iCloud Screen

Figure 11: Passcode Creation Screen

6. Navigating the Screens

There are many ways to navigate the iPhone. Use the following tips to quickly navigate the screens of the iPhone:

- Use the **Home** button to return to the Home screen at any time. Any application or tool that you were using will be in the same state when you return to it.
- At the Home screen, slide your finger to the left to access additional pages. If nothing happens, the other pages are blank.

- Touch the center of the Home screen and slide your finger down to access the iPhone's search feature. You may search any data stored on your phone, including application data.

7. Organizing Icons

You may wish to re-order the location of the application icons on the screens. To organize application icons:

1. Touch an icon and hold it until all of the icons begin to shake. The icons can now be moved around the screen.
2. Move the icon to the desired location and let go of the screen. The icon is relocated and the surrounding icons are re-ordered accordingly. If an icon that used to be on the screen is gone, then it has been moved to a different Home screen in the process.
3. To move an icon to another screen, move the icon to the edge of the current one and hold it there. The adjacent screen appears. Drop the icon in the desired location.
4. Press the **Home** button. The icons stop shaking.

8. Creating an Icon Folder

When there are many icons on the Home screens, you may wish to organize the icons into folders. Each folder can have a meaningful name to enable you to find the icons easily. To create a folder:

1. Touch an icon and hold it until all of the icons begin to shake. The icons can now be moved.
2. Move one icon on top of another and let go of the screen. A folder with those two icons is created, as shown in **Figure 12**. Touch the ⊗ button to enter a name for the folder.
3. Enter a name for the folder and touch **Done**. The new name is saved.
4. To exit the folder, touch anywhere outside of it. The folder closes.
5. Press the **Home** button. The icons stop shaking.

Note: To add more icons to a folder, just touch an icon while it is shaking and move it onto the folder.

Figure 12: A New Folder on the iPhone

9. Using Wi-Fi

Use a nearby Wi-Fi hotspot or a home router to avoid having to use data. Wi-Fi is required to download large applications and to use FaceTime. To turn on Wi-Fi:

1. Touch the ![icon] icon. The Settings screen appears, as shown in **Figure 13**.
2. Touch **Wi-Fi**. The Wi-Fi Networks screen appears, as shown in **Figure 14**.

3. Touch the ⬭ switch next to 'Wi-Fi'. Wi-Fi turns on and a list of available networks appears, as shown in **Figure 15**. If the network has an 🔒 icon next to it, a password is needed to connect to it.

4. Touch the network to which you would like to connect. The Wi-Fi Password prompt appears if the network is protected, as shown in **Figure 16**.

5. Enter the network password. Touch **Join** in the bottom right-hand corner of the screen. Provided that you entered the correct password, a check mark appears next to the network name and the 📶 icon appears at the top of the screen. You are connected to the Wi-Fi network.

Note: If you enter an incorrect password, the message "Unable to join the network >Network Name<" appears, where '>Network Name<' is the name of your network. The network password is usually written on the modem given to you by your internet service provider. It is sometimes called a WEP Key.

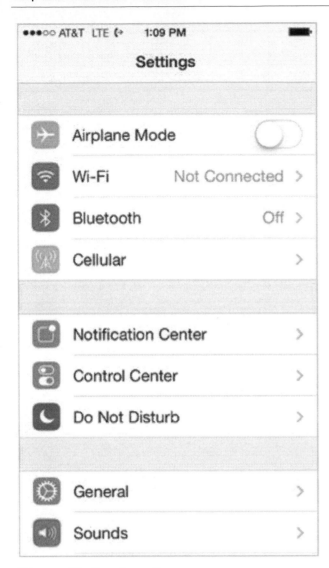

Figure 13: Settings Screen

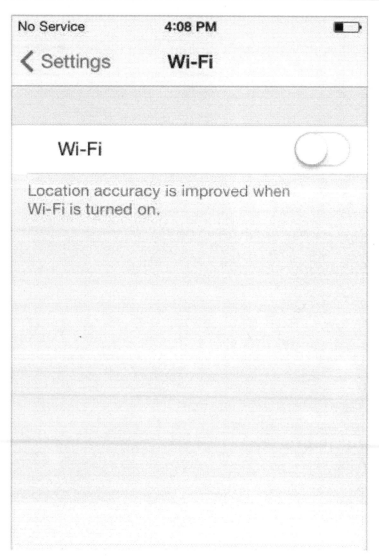

Figure 14: Wi-Fi Networks Screen

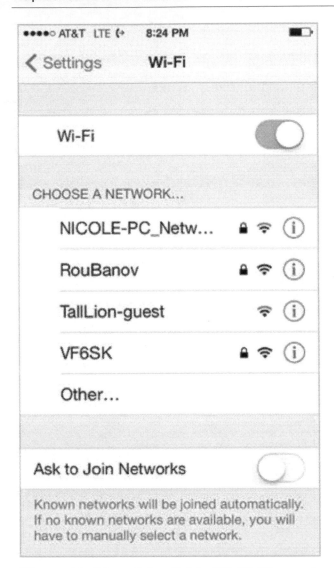

Figure 15: List of Available Wi-Fi Networks

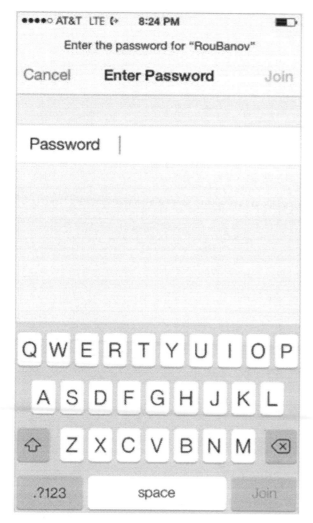

Figure 16: Wi-Fi Password Prompt

10. Accessing Quick Settings through the Control Center

There are various settings that you can access without opening the Settings screen by using the Control Center. To use the control center:

1. Touch the bottom of the screen at any time and slide your finger up. The Control Center appears, as shown in **Figure 17**.
2. Touch one of the following icons at the top of the Control Center to turn on the corresponding function:

✈ - Turns Airplane mode on or off.

- Turns Wi-Fi on or off.

 - Turns Bluetooth on or off.

 - Turns 'Do not disturb' on or off.

 - Turns automatic screen rotation on or off.

A white icon, such as a icon, indicates that the function is turned on.

3. Touch one of the following icons at the bottom of the Control Center to turn on the corresponding service:

 - Turns the flashlight on or off.

 - Opens the timer application.

 - Opens the calculator application.

 - Turns on the camera.

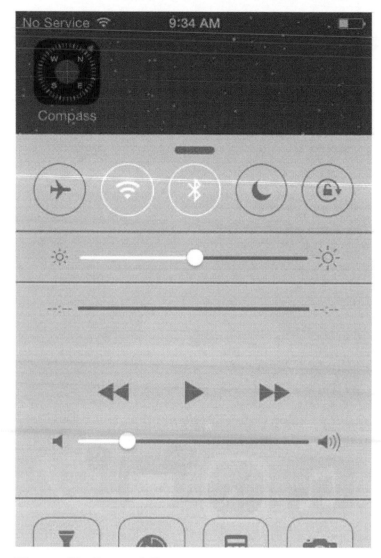

Figure 17: Control Center

11. Using the Notification Center

The Notification Center shows event reminders and all types of alerts, such as calendar events, received texts, and missed calls. To open the notification center, touch the top of the screen at any time and move your finger down. Touch a notification to open the corresponding application. For instance, touch a calendar event to open the calendar. You can also touch **All** or **Missed** at the top of the screen to view the corresponding notifications.

Making Voice and Video Calls

Table of Contents

1. Dialing a Number

Numbers that are not in your Phonebook can be dialed on the keypad. To manually dial a phone number, touch the [icon] icon on the Home screen. The keypad appears, as shown in **Figure 1**. Touch the [icon] icon at the bottom of the screen, if you do not see the keypad. Enter the desired phone number and then touch **CALL** at the bottom of the screen. The iPhone dials the number.

Note: If an incorrect number is entered, "Error Performing Request - Unknown Error" appears.

Figure 1: Keypad

2. Calling a Contact

If a number is stored in your Phonebook, you may touch the name of a contact to dial it. To call a contact already stored in your iPhone:

1. Touch the icon on the Home screen. The Phonebook appears, as shown in **Figure 2**.
2. Touch the name of the desired contact. The Contact Information screen appears, as shown in **Figure 3**.
3. Touch the desired phone number. The iPhone calls the contact's number. Refer to *"Managing Contacts"* on page 51 to learn more about adding or removing contacts.

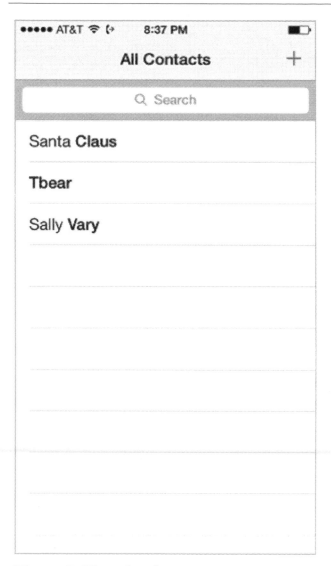

Figure 2: Phonebook

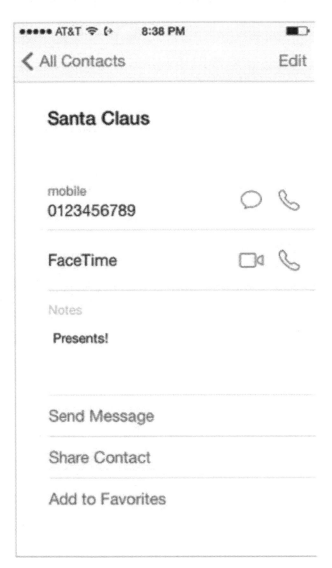

Figure 3: Contact Information Screen

3. Calling a Favorite

There is no Speed Dial feature on the iPhone. Instead, frequently dialed numbers can be saved as Favorites, which can be accessed more quickly than other contacts. To call a number stored in Favorites:

1. Touch the ![phone icon] icon on the Home screen. The keypad screen appears.

2. Touch the ![star icon] icon at the bottom of the screen. The Favorites screen appears, as shown in **Figure 4**.

3. Touch the name of a Favorite. The iPhone calls the selected number. Refer to *"Managing Contacts"* on page 51 to learn more about managing Favorites.

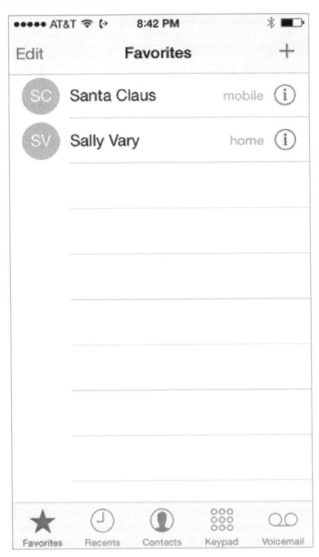

Figure 4: Favorites Screen

4. Returning a Recent Phone Call

After missing a call, your iPhone will notify you of who called and at what time. The iPhone also shows a history of all recently placed calls. To view and return a missed call or redial a recently entered number:

1. Touch the [icon] icon on the Home screen. The Calling screen appears.

2. Touch the ⏰ icon at the bottom of the screen. The Recent Calls screen appears, with the most recent calls on top. Missed or declined calls are shown in red. The 📞 icon is shown next to a placed call, as outlined in **Figure 5**.
3. Touch the name of a contact. The iPhone dials the contact.

Note: To view only missed calls, touch **MISSED** *at the top of the Recent Calls screen.*

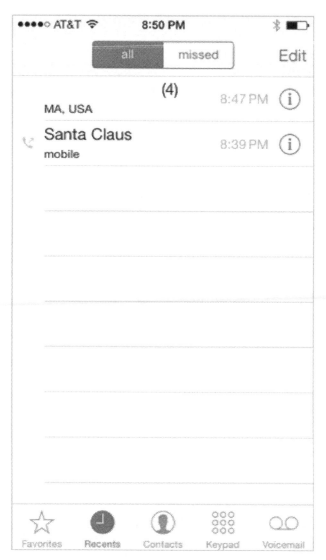

Figure 5: Recent Calls Screen

5. Receiving a Voice Call

There are several ways to accept or reject a voice call based on whether or not the screen is locked. Use the following tips when receiving a voice call:

- To receive an incoming voice call while the iPhone is locked, touch and move the on the slider, shown in **Figure 6**, to the right. The call is answered.
- To mute the ringer, press the Sleep/Wake button. To reject the incoming call, press the Sleep/Wake button again.
- To receive an incoming call while using an application (or viewing a Home screen), touch **ANSWER**, as shown in **Figure 7**. To reject the incoming call, touch **DECLINE**. The call is declined. The number then shows up in red in the list of recent calls, signifying that it is a missed call, and a notification appears above the icon on the Home screen.
- Touch **Message** or **Remind Me** to decline a call if you are currently busy but wish to address it later. Refer to *"Replying to an Incoming Call with a Text Message"* on page 42 or *"Setting a Reminder to Return an Incoming Call"* on page 43 to learn more about these options.

Figure 6: Incoming Call, iPhone Locked

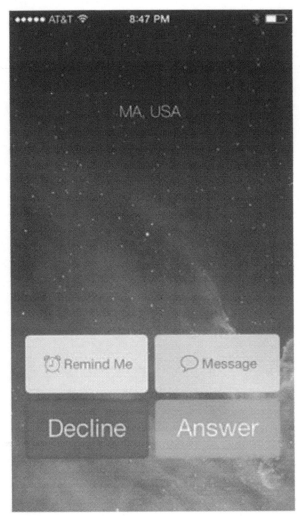

Figure 7: Incoming Call, iPhone Unlocked

6. Replying to an Incoming Call with a Text Message

During an incoming call, you may reject it and automatically send a text message to the caller. To reply to an incoming call with a text message:

1. Touch **Message** during an incoming voice call. A list of pre-defined text messages appear.
2. Touch a message. The selected text message is sent to the caller. Alternatively, touch **Custom** to enter your own text message.
3. Touch the **Send** button. The iPhone sends the custom text message to the caller.

7. Setting a Reminder to Return an Incoming Call

During an incoming call, you may reject it and automatically set a reminder for yourself to return the call at a specified time or when you reach a specific location (such as work or home). To set a reminder to return an incoming call, touch **Remind Me** during an incoming voice call. The following reminder options appear: 'In 1 hour' and 'When I leave'. Touch **In 1 hour**. The iPhone displays a pop-up after one hour has passed reminding you to call back. Alternatively, touch **When I leave** to have the iPhone remind you when you leave your current location.

8. Using the Speakerphone During a Voice Call

The iPhone has a built-in Speakerphone, which is useful when calling from a car or when several people need to hear the conversation. To use the Speakerphone during a phone call:

1. Place a voice call. The Calling Screen appears, as shown in **Figure 8**.

2. Touch the 🔊 icon. The Speakerphone is turned on. Adjust the volume of the Speakerphone by using the Volume Controls. Refer to *"Button Layout"* on page 9 to locate the Volume Controls.

3. Touch the 🔊 icon. The Speakerphone is turned off.

Figure 8: Calling Screen

9. Using the Keypad During a Voice Call

You may wish to use the keypad while on a call in order to input numbers in an automated menu or to enter an account number. To use the keypad during a phone call, place a voice call and touch the ▦ icon. The keypad appears. To hide the keypad again, touch **Hide Keypad**.

10. Using the Mute Function During a Voice Call

During a voice call, you may wish to mute your side of the conversation. When mute is turned on, the person on the other end of the line will not hear anything on your side. To use Mute during a call, place a voice call and touch the ![icon] icon. The iPhone mutes your voice and the caller(s) can no longer hear you, but you are still able to hear them. Touch the ![icon] icon. Mute is turned off.

11. Putting a Caller on Hold (hidden button)

Apple replaced the Hold button (![icon]) with the ![icon] button on the iPhone 4 and later generations. However, the Hold function still exists. Press and hold the ![icon] button while on a call until the ![icon] button appears. Release the screen. The call is put on hold.

12. Starting a Conference Call (Adding a Call)

To talk to more than one person at a time, call another person while continuing the current call. To create a conference call, place a voice call and then touch the ![icon] icon. The list of contacts or the keypad is shown. Dial a number or select a contact to call. The first contact is put on hold while the iPhone dials and connects to the second. Touch the ![icon] icon. A three-way conference call is created, as shown in **Figure 9**.

Note: Up to six lines may be included in a conference call.

Figure 9: Three-Way Conference Call

13. Starting a Facetime Call

The iPhone 5S has the ability to place a video call to another iPhone (generation 4 or later), iPad, Mac, or iPod (third generation and on). Starting with the iPhone 5, Facetime does not require a Wi-Fi connection and you can place and receive calls using a 4G connection (provided that you have at least one bar of service). However, using Wi-Fi may still provide a better video calling experience. You may also place a Facetime voice call if you do not wish to use the camera. Refer to *"Using Wi-Fi"* on page 24 to learn how to turn it on. To place a Facetime call:

1. Touch the icon on the Home screen. The keypad appears.

2. Touch **Contacts** at the bottom of the screen. The Phonebook appears.
3. Touch the name of a contact. The contact information screen appears.

4. Touch the ▭◁ icon to place a FaceTime call with video, or touch the ☎ icon to place a FaceTime call with only audio. A Facetime call is placed. A high-pitched beeping sound plays until the call connects.

5. Touch the 🔄 button at any time to switch cameras, as outlined in **Figure 10**. Using this feature, you can either show your contact what you are seeing or show them your face.

The iPhone 5S can also receive FaceTime calls. To receive an incoming FaceTime call, touch the [◀ Accept] button, as outlined in **Figure 11**.

Note: Calling a device that is not compatible with FaceTime or calling a contact that is currently unavailable will result in an error, as shown in **Figure 12**.

Figure 10: Switch Camera Icon

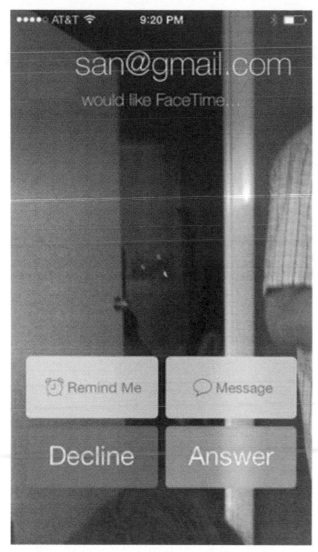

Figure 11: Receiving a FaceTime Call

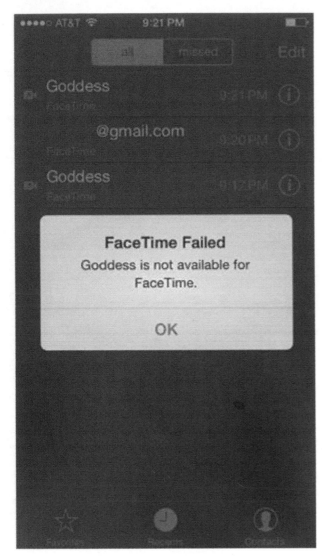

Figure 12: FaceTime Call Error

Managing Contacts

Table of Contents

1. Adding a New Contact

The iPhone can store phone numbers, email addresses, and other Contact Information in its Phonebook. To add a new contact to the Phonebook:

Note: For some unexplained reason, Apple has decided to place the Contacts icon in the Extras folder by default. If you cannot find it, look in that folder.

1. Touch the ![icon] icon on the Home screen. The Phonebook appears.
2. Touch the ┼ button in the upper right-hand corner of the screen. The New Contact screen appears, as shown in **Figure 1**.
3. Touch **First**. The keyboard appears. Enter the first name of the contact.
4. Touch **Last**. Enter the last name of the contact.
5. Touch **add phone**. The keypad appears. Enter the contact's phone number. The number is entered.
6. Touch any empty field to enter the desired information, and then touch **Done** in the upper right-hand corner of the screen. The contact's information is stored.

Note: Refer to "Tips and Tricks" on page 294 to learn how to add an extension after the contact's phone number.

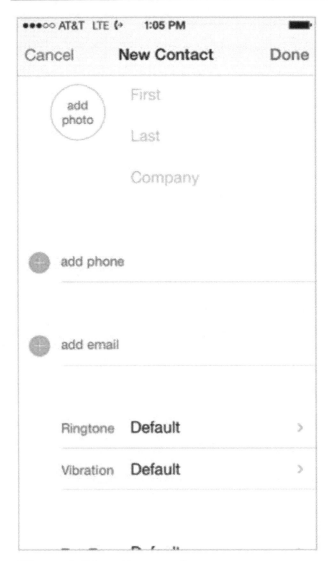

Figure 1: New Contact Screen

2. Finding a Contact

After adding contacts to your iPhone's Phonebook, you may search for them. To find a stored contact:

1. Touch the ![icon] icon on the Home screen. The Phonebook appears.
2. Touch **Search** at the top of the screen. The keyboard appears.
3. Start typing the name of a contact. Contact matches appear as you type, as shown in **Figure 2**.
4. Touch a match. The Contact Info screen appears, as shown in **Figure 3**.

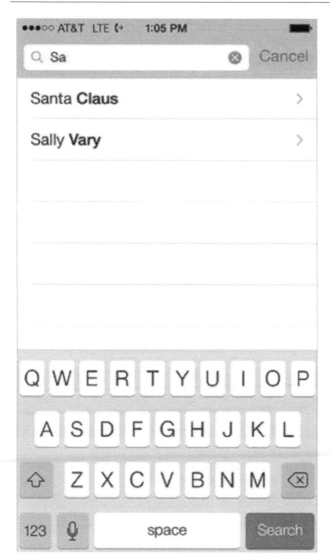

Figure 2: Contact Matches

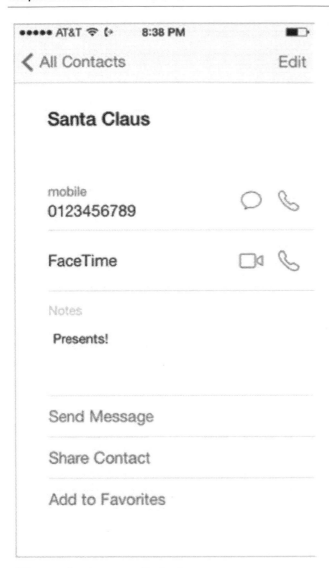

Figure 3: Contact Info Screen

3. Deleting a Contact

You may delete contact information from your Phonebook in order to free up space or for organizational purposes. To delete unwanted contact information:

Warning: There is no way to restore contact information after it has been deleted.

1. Touch the ![icon] icon on the Home screen. The Phonebook appears. If a list of all contacts does not appear, touch **All Contacts** in the upper left-hand corner of the screen to view the list.

2. Find and touch the name of the contact that you wish to delete. The Contact Info screen appears. Refer to *"Finding a Contact"* on page 52 to learn how to search for a contact.
3. Touch **Edit** in the upper right-hand corner of the screen. The Contact Information Editing screen appears.
4. Touch **Delete Contact** at the bottom of the screen, as outlined in **Figure 4**. A Confirmation menu appears.
5. Touch **Delete Contact** again. The contact's information is deleted and will no longer appear in your Phonebook.

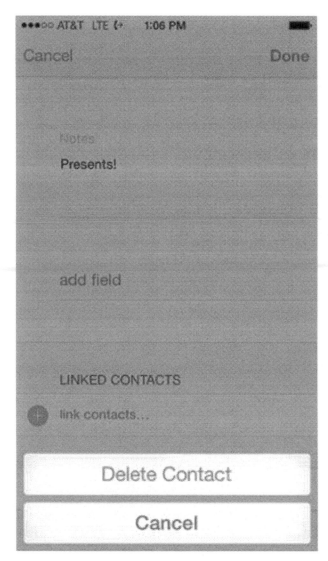

Figure 4: Delete Contact Screen

4. Editing Contact Information

After adding contacts to your Phonebook, you may edit them at any time. To edit an existing contact's information:

1. Touch the ![icon] icon on the Home screen. The Phonebook appears. If a list of all contacts does not appear, touch **All Contacts** in the upper left-hand corner of the screen to view the list.
2. Find and touch a contact's name. The Contact Info screen appears. Refer to *"Finding a Contact"* on page 52 to learn how to search for a contact.
3. Touch **Edit** in the upper right-hand corner of the screen. The Contact Editing screen appears.
4. Touch a field to edit the corresponding information. Touch **Done** in the upper right-hand corner of the screen. The contact's information is updated.

5. Sharing a Contact's Information

To share a contact's information with someone else:

1. Touch the ![icon] icon. The Phonebook appears. If a list of all contacts does not appear, touch **All Contacts** in the upper left-hand corner of the screen to view the list.
2. Find and touch a contact's name. The Contact Info screen appears. Refer to *"Finding a Contact"* on page 52 to learn how.
3. Touch **Share Contact** at the bottom of the screen. The Sharing Options menu appears at the bottom of the screen, as shown in **Figure 5**.
4. Follow the steps in the appropriate section on the following page to email or text the contact's information.

To send the contact's information via email:

1. Touch the ![icon] icon in the Sharing Options menu. The New Email screen appears, as shown in **Figure 6**. Choose one of the following options for entering the email address:

    *   Start typing the name of the contact with whom you wish to share the information. The matching contacts appear. Touch the contact's name. The contact's email address is added.

- Enter the email address from scratch. To use a number, touch **_123** at the bottom left of the screen. When done, touch the **return** button in the lower right-hand corner of the screen. Enter more addresses if needed.

- Touch the ⊕ icon to select as many contacts from your Phonebook or enter as many email addresses as you wish.

2. Enter an optional subject by touching **Subject**, and touch **CC** to add other addresses to which to send the information.
3. Touch **Send** in the upper right-hand corner of the screen. The contact's information is sent to the selected email addresses.

To send a contact's information via multimedia message, touch the ⬤ icon in the Sharing Options menu. The New Message screen appears, as shown in **Figure 7**. Enter a phone number or phone numbers and touch **Send**. The contact's information is sent. There are three methods for entering the phone number:

- Start typing the name of the contact with whom you wish to share the information. Matching contacts appear. Touch the contact's name. The contact's number is added.

- Type the phone number from scratch. To use numbers, touch the [_123] button at the bottom left of the screen. When done, touch the [return] button in the lower right-hand corner of the screen.

- Touch the ⊕ icon to select one or more contacts from the Phonebook.

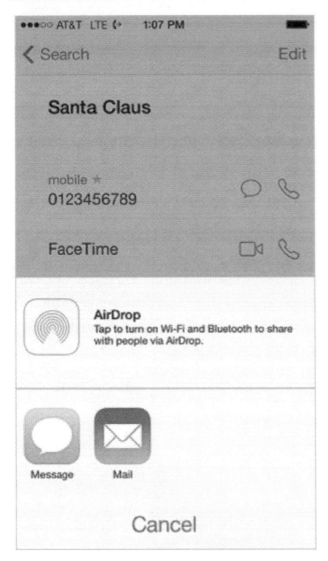

Figure 5: Sharing Options Menu

Figure 6: New Email Screen

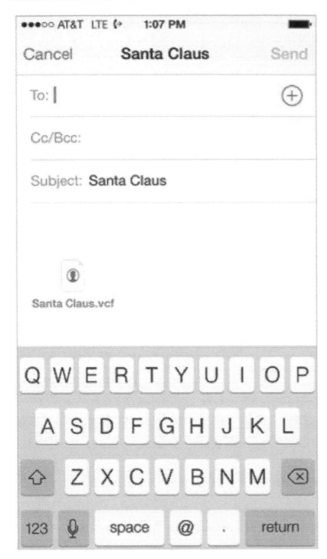

Figure 7: New Message Screen

6. Adding a Contact to Favorites (Speed Dial)

The iPhone has no Speed Dial feature, but the most frequently dialed numbers can be stored as Favorites, which can be accessed more quickly. To add a contact to Favorites:

1. Touch the ![icon] icon on the Home screen. The Phonebook appears. If a list of all contacts does not appear, touch **All Contacts** in the upper left-hand corner of the screen to view the list.

2. Find and touch the contact's name. The Contact Info screen appears. Refer to *"Finding a Contact"* on page 52 to learn search for a contact.

3. Touch **Add to Favorites** at the bottom of the screen. If more than one number is stored for the contact, a menu appears at the bottom of the screen asking you which number should be added. You may also receive a prompt asking you whether the phone should dial the phone number or place a FaceTime called when the favorite is selected.

4. Select the desired number, if applicable, and select the phone or FaceTime number. The contact is added to Favorites. Refer to *"Viewing Favorite Contacts"* on page 61 to learn how to view Favorites.

7. Viewing Favorite Contacts

After adding contacts to Favorites, you may view them at any time. To view your Favorites:

1. Touch the [icon] icon on the Home screen. The keypad appears.

2. Touch the [icon] icon at the bottom left-hand corner of the screen. The Favorites screen appears, as shown in **Figure 8**. Beside the name of each Favorite is the type of number (i.e. home, mobile, etc.) written in gray letters.

3. Touch the name of a Favorite contact. The iPhone calls the number.

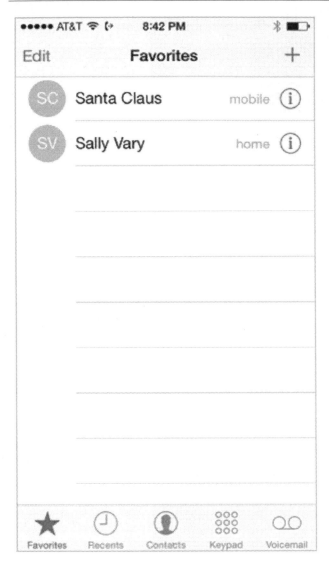

Figure 8: Favorites Screen

8. Removing a Favorite Contact from the List

You may delete a Favorite contact to free up space in your Favorites list. To delete an unwanted Favorite:

1. Open the Favorites screen. Refer to *"Viewing Favorite Contacts"* on page 61 to learn how.

2. Touch **Edit** in the upper left-hand corner of the screen. A ⊖ button appears to the left of each favorite.

3. Touch the ⊖ button next to the Favorite you wish to delete. 'Delete' appears to the right of the corresponding name, as outlined in **Figure 9**.

4. Touch **Delete**. The Favorite is erased.

Note: Touch and hold the ≡ *icon to the right of a Favorite's name to move it. Drag the Favorite to the desired location in the list.*

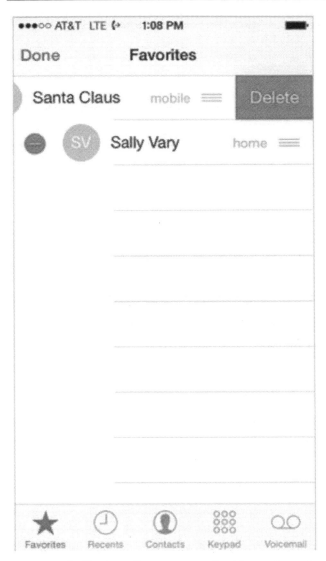

Figure 9: Delete Button on the Favorites Screen

9. Changing the Contact Sort Order

By default, the iPhone sorts the contacts in the Phonebook by last name. For instance, if the names Jane Doe and John Johnson are in the list, John Johnson would come after Jane Doe because 'J' comes after 'D' in the English alphabet. To change the sort order:

1. Touch the ![icon] icon. The Settings screen appears, as shown in **Figure 10**.
2. Touch **Mail, Contacts, Calendars**. The Mail, Contacts, Calendars screen appears, as shown in **Figure 11**.

3. Touch **Sort Order** at the bottom of the screen. The Sort Order screen appears, as shown in **Figure 12**.
4. Touch **First, Last**. A check mark appears to the right of the option and the contacts will be sorted by first name.
5. Touch **Last, First**. A check mark appears to the right of the option and the contacts will be sorted by last name.

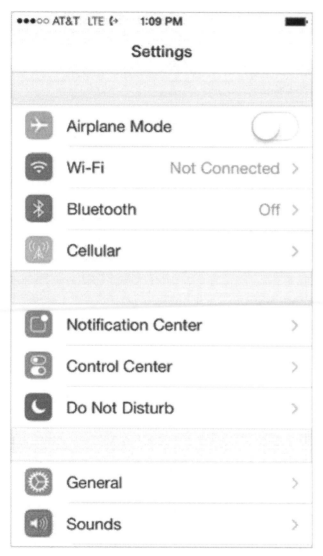

Figure 10: Settings Screen

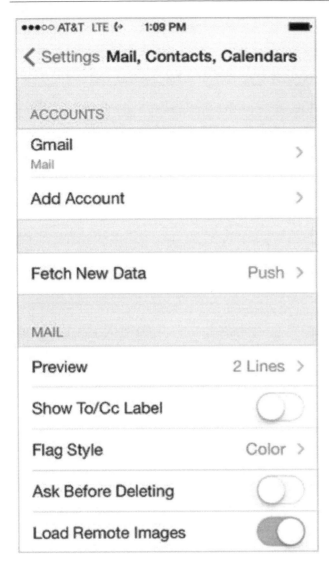

Figure 11: Mail, Contacts, Calendars Screen

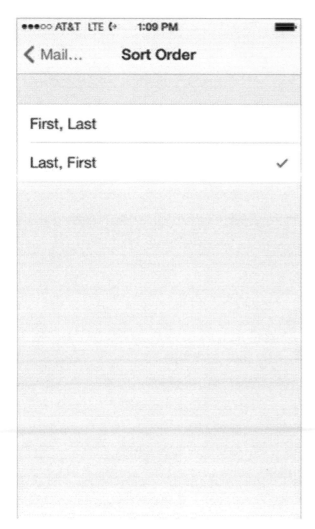

Figure 12: Sort Order Screen

Text Messaging

Table of Contents

1. Composing a New Text Message

The iPhone can send text messages to other mobile phones. To compose a new message:

1. Touch the icon on the Home screen. The Messages screen appears, as shown in **Figure 1**.

2. Touch the icon in the upper right-hand corner of the screen. The New Message screen appears, as shown in **Figure 2**.

3. Enter the phone number of the recipient. There are three options for entering this information:

    - Start typing the name of the contact. Matching contacts appear as you type. Touch the contact's name. The contact's number is added.
    - Enter the phone number from scratch.
    - Touch the button to select a contact from the Phonebook. Add as many numbers as desired.

4. Touch the text field. The cursor starts flashing at the beginning of the field.

5. Enter your message. If you begin to type a word incorrectly, the iPhone may give you a suggestion. To accept the suggestion, touch **Space**. To reject it, touch the key to the right of the suggestion.

6. Touch **Send** when finished entering the message. The message is sent. The iPhone shows the progress of the message at the top of the screen. When it is finished sending, a sound is played or the phone vibrates. Your message is shown in a green bubble on the right side of the screen, as shown in **Figure 3**. All text messages are shown in conversation view.

To send a new message to someone you have already texted:

1. Touch the icon on the Home screen. The Messages screen appears.

2. Touch the name or number of the recipient. The Conversation screen appears. If the name is not in the list, try scrolling down by touching the screen and moving your finger up. If you cannot find the name, you may have deleted your conversation with that contact.

3. Touch the text field. The cursor starts flashing and a keyboard is shown.

4. Enter the message and then touch **Send**. The message is sent. The most recent message is shown in a green bubble at the bottom right of the conversation. Touch the screen and move your finger down to scroll through older messages.

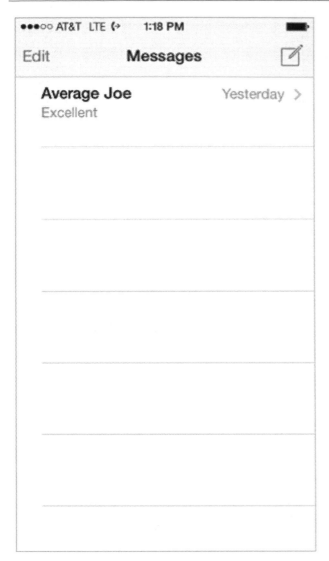

Figure 1: Messages Screen

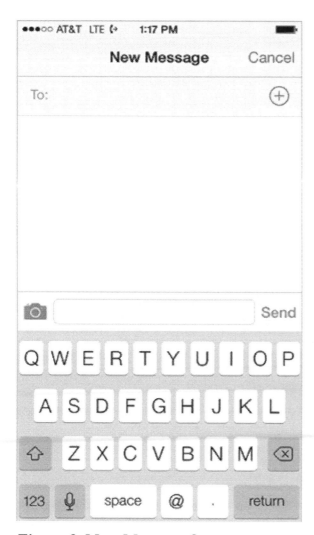

Figure 2: New Message Screen

Figure 3: Your Message in a Green Bubble

2. Copying, Cutting, and Pasting Text

The iPhone allows you to copy or cut text from one location and paste it to another. Copying leaves the text in its current location and allows you to paste it elsewhere. Cutting deletes the text from its current location and allows you to paste it elsewhere. To cut, copy, and paste text:

1. Touch text in a text field or in a conversation. The Select menu appears above the text, as shown in **Figure 4**. Refer to *"Composing a New Text Message"* on page 68 to learn how to compose a text.
2. Touch **Select All**. All of the text is selected. To select a single word, touch **Select**. Blue dots appear around the word or phrase.
3. Touch and hold one of the blue dots and drag it in any direction. The text between the dots is highlighted and a text menu appears, as shown in **Figure 5**.
4. Touch **Cut** or **Copy**. The corresponding action is taken and the text is ready to be pasted.
5. Touch and hold any empty text field, and then touch **Paste**. The text is inserted.

Note: Refer to "Tips and Tricks" *on page 294 to learn more about editing text.*

Figure 4: Select Menu

Figure 5: Text Menu

3. Using the Spell Check Feature

The iPhone will underline words that are spelled incorrectly with a red dotted line. Touch the underlined word once to see spelling suggestions. Touch a suggestion to substitute the word immediately. If auto-correction is enabled, the iPhone will automatically replace common typos. Over time, the iPhone will learn your most commonly typed words, even names and slang. Refer to *"Adjusting Language and Keyboard Settings"* on page 225 to learn more about auto-correction.

4. Receiving a Text Message

The iPhone can receive text messages from any other mobile device. When the iPhone receives a text, the phone vibrates once or plays a sound, depending on the settings. The New Message notification appears on the Home screen, as shown in **Figure 6**, on the lock screen, as shown in **Figure 7**, or in the Notification Bar at the top of the screen, as outlined in **Figure 8**. Whether the notification appears in the Notification Bar or on the Home screen depends on your settings. Use the following tips when receiving text messages:

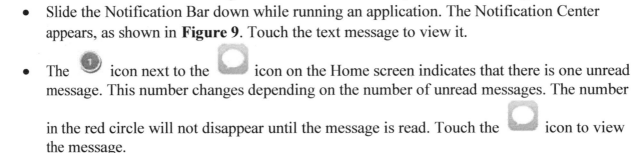

- Slide the icon to the right on the Lock screen to open the text message.
- Slide the Notification Bar down while running an application. The Notification Center appears, as shown in **Figure 9**. Touch the text message to view it.

- The icon next to the icon on the Home screen indicates that there is one unread message. This number changes depending on the number of unread messages. The number in the red circle will not disappear until the message is read. Touch the icon to view the message.
- Touch **Reply** to send a text back to the contact. The Conversation screen appears.
- Touch **Close** to reply later.

Note: Refer to "Composing a New Text Message" *on page 68 to learn more about sending text messages.*

Figure 6: New Message Notification on the Home Screen

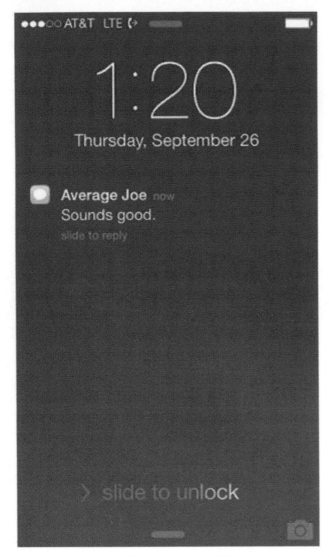

Figure 7: New Message Notification on the Lock Screen

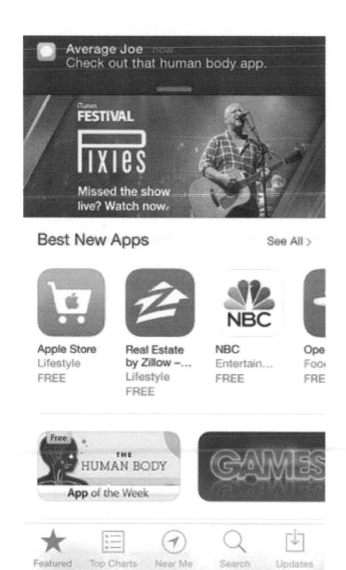

Figure 8: New Message Notification in the Notification Bar

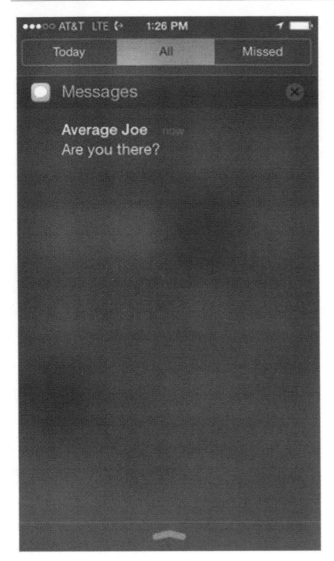

Figure 9: Notification Center

5. Reading a Stored Text Message

You may read any text messages that you have received, provided that you have not deleted them. To read stored text messages:

1. Touch the [icon] icon on the Home screen. The Messages screen appears. The iPhone organizes conversations based on the date the last message in the conversation was sent or received, with the most recent conversation at the top of the list.
2. Touch the name of a contact to view the conversation. The Conversation screen appears.

3. Touch the screen and move your finger up or down to scroll through the conversation. The most recent messages appear at the bottom.
4. Touch **Messages** in the upper left-hand corner of the screen. The Messages screen appears.

6. Forwarding a Text Message

You may wish to forward a text message. To forward a text message:

1. Touch the ⬜ icon on the Home screen. The Messages screen appears, displaying each sender's name on the left and the date of the message on the right.
2. Touch the conversation that contains the message(s) that you wish to forward. The Conversation screen appears.
3. Touch **Edit** in the upper right-hand corner of the screen. A gray circle appears to the left of each individual message.
4. Touch each message(s) that you wish to forward. Every time a message is selected, a blue check mark appears in the gray circle, as shown in **Figure 10**.
5. Touch the ⤵ button at the bottom of the screen. The New Message screen appears.
6. Start typing the name of a contact or touch the ⊕ icon to select a number from the Phonebook. The contact is added to the Addressee list.
7. Touch **Send**. The message is forwarded to the contacts in the Addressee list.

Figure 10: Selected Messages

7. Calling the Sender from within a Text

After receiving a text message from a contact, you may call that person without ever exiting the text message. To call someone from whom you have received a text message:

1. Touch the [icon] icon on the Home screen. The Messages screen appears. The iPhone organizes conversations based on the date the last message in the conversation was sent or received, with the most recent conversation at the top of the list.
2. Touch the conversation that contains the message(s) from the sender you wish to call. The Conversation screen appears.
3. Touch [icon] at the top of the screen. The iPhone places the call.

8. Viewing Sender Information from within a Text

If you have stored a contact's information in the Phonebook, you may view it at any time without leaving a text conversation between the two of you. To view the information of a contact who sent you a message:

1. Touch the [icon] icon on the Home screen. The Messages screen appears. The iPhone organizes conversations based on the date the last message in the conversation was sent or received, with the most recent conversation at the top of the list.
2. Touch a conversation. The Conversation screen appears.
3. Touch the screen and move your finger down until the top of the conversation appears.
4. Touch **Contact** in the upper right-hand corner of the screen. The contact's information is displayed.
5. Touch the contact's name in the upper left-hand corner of the screen, as outlined in red in **Figure 11**. The iPhone returns to the conversation.

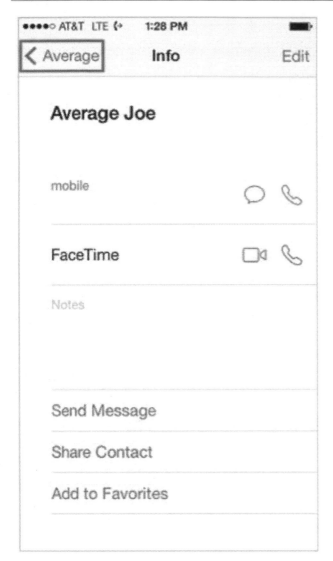

Figure 11: Contact Information Screen

9. Deleting a Text Message

The iPhone can delete separate text messages or an entire conversation, which is a series of text messages between you and a contact.

Warning: Once deleted, text messages cannot be restored.

To delete an entire conversation:

1. Touch the ⬜ icon on the Home screen. The Messages screen appears. The iPhone organizes conversations based on the date the last message in the conversation was sent or received, with the most recent conversation at the top of the list.

2. Touch **Edit** in the upper left-hand corner of the screen. A ⊖ button appears to the left of each name, as shown in **Figure 12**. If 'Messages' is shown at the top left of the screen, touch **Messages** to return to the Messages screen, and then touch **Edit**.

3. Touch the ⊖ button next to a conversation. **Delete** appears next to the contact's name on the right side of the screen.

4. Touch **Delete**. The entire conversation is deleted.

To delete a separate text message:

1. Touch the ⬜ icon on the Home screen. The Messages screen appears.
2. Touch a conversation. The Conversation screen appears.
3. Touch **Edit** in the upper right-hand corner of the screen. A gray circle appears to the left of each individual message.
4. Touch as many separate messages as desired. A blue check mark appears in the circle next to each message that you select.
5. Touch **Delete** at the bottom of the screen. The selected messages are deleted.

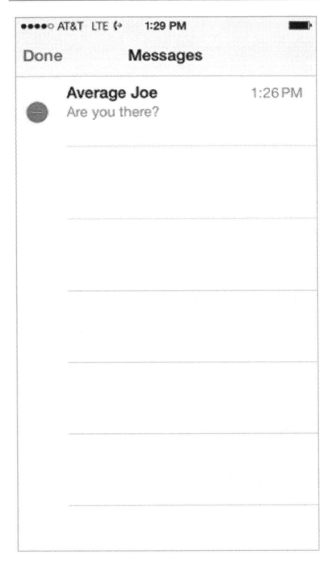

Figure 12: Delete Buttons

10. Adding Texted Phone Numbers to the Phonebook

A phone number sent via text message can be added to your Phonebook immediately. To add a texted phone number to your Phonebook:

1. Touch the icon on the Home screen. The Messages screen appears.
2. Touch a conversation. The Conversation screen appears.
3. Touch the blue arrow next to the phone number in the conversation. The Save Number menu appears, as shown in **Figure 13**.
4. Touch **Create New Contact**. The New Contact screen appears, with the phone number field filled in, as shown in **Figure 14**.
5. Touch **First** and enter a first name. Touch **Last** and enter a last name. Touch **Done** in the upper right-hand corner of the screen. The contact is added to your Phonebook.

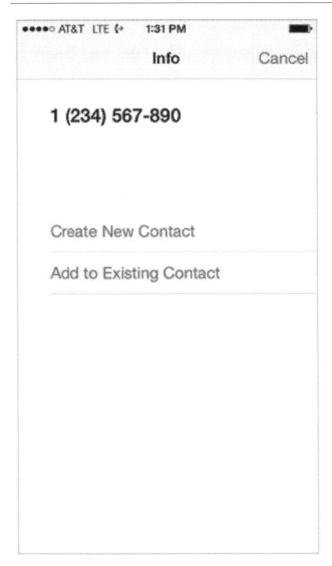

Figure 13: Save Number Menu

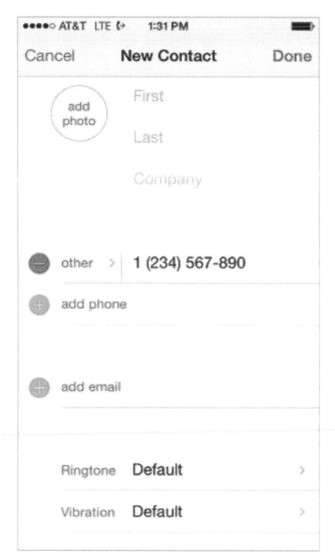

Figure 14: New Contact Screen

11. Sending a Picture Message

You may attach a picture to any text message you send.

To send a picture message:

1. Touch the ⬜ icon on the Home screen. The Messages screen appears.

2. Touch the [icon] icon. The New Message screen appears.

3. Touch the [button] button to the left of the text field. The Photo Attachment menu appears as shown in **Figure 15**.

4. Follow the steps in one of the sections below to either attach an existing picture or take a picture to send:

To attach an existing picture to the text message:

1. Touch **Choose Existing**. A list of Photo Albums appears, as shown in **Figure 16**.
2. Touch a photo. The preview of the photo appears.
3. Touch **Choose**. The photo is attached to the text message.

To take a picture and attach it to the text message:

1. Touch **Take Photo or Video**. The camera turns on, as shown in **Figure 17**.
2. Touch the [button] button at the bottom of the screen. The photo is captured and a preview of the photo appears.
3. Touch **Use** to use the photo in the message or touch **Retake** to discard the picture and take another one. The photo is attached.
4. Touch **Send**. The picture message is sent.

Note: Up to nine photos may be sent in a picture message.

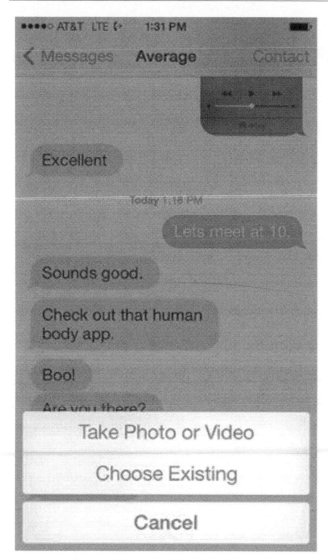

Figure 15: Photo Attachment Menu

Figure 16: List of Photo Albums

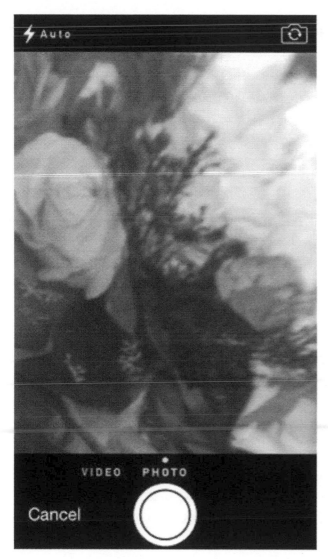

Figure 17: Camera Turned On

Using the Safari Web Browser

Table of Contents

---

1. Navigating to a Website

You can surf the web using your iPhone. To navigate to a website using the web address:

1. Touch the ![icon] icon on the Home screen. The Safari Web browser opens.
2. Touch the Address bar at the top of the screen, as outlined in **Figure 1**. The keyboard appears. . If you do not see the Address bar, touch the screen and move your finger down to scroll up.
3. Touch the ![button] button. The address field is erased.
4. Enter a web address and touch **Go**. Safari navigates to the website.
5. Touch the ![button] button. Safari navigates to the previous web page.
6. Touch the ![button] button. Safari navigates to the next web page.

Figure 1: Address Bar in Safari

2. Adding and Viewing Bookmarks

The iPhone can store favorite websites as Bookmarks to allow you to access them faster in the future. To add a Bookmark in Safari:

1. Touch the ![icon] icon on the Home screen. The Safari browser opens.
2. Navigate to a website. Refer to *"Navigating to a Website"* on page 94 to learn how.

3. Touch the ⬆️ button at the bottom of the screen. The Bookmark menu appears, as shown in **Figure 2**.
4. Touch **Bookmark**. The Add Bookmark window appears, as shown in **Figure 3**.
5. Enter a name for the bookmark and touch **Save** in the top right-hand corner of the screen. The website is added to the Bookmarks.

Note: To view saved Bookmarks, touch the 📖 *icon at the bottom of the screen in the Safari browser. The Bookmarks screen appears, as shown in* **Figure 4**. *Touch a bookmark. Safari navigates to the indicated website.*

Figure 2: Bookmark Menu

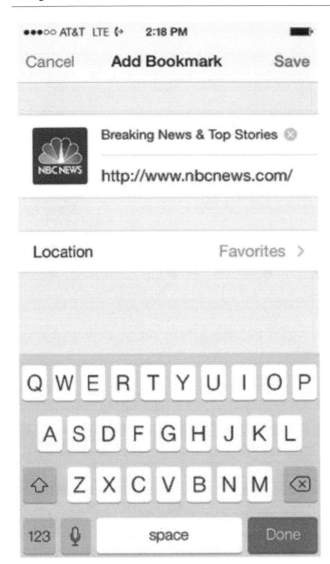

Figure 3: Add Bookmark Window

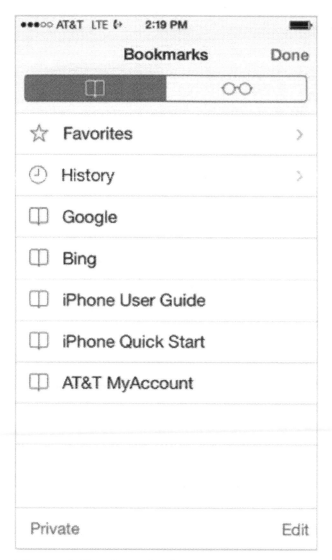

Figure 4: Bookmarks Screen

3. Adding a Bookmark to the Home Screen

On the iPhone, bookmarks can be added to the Home screen; they will then appear like application icons. To add a bookmark to the Home screen as an icon:

1. Touch the icon on the Home screen. The Safari browser opens.
2. Navigate to a website. Refer to *"Navigating to a Website"* on page 94 to learn how.

3. Touch the button at the bottom of the screen. The Bookmark menu appears.
4. Touch **Add to Home Screen**. The Add to Home window appears, as shown in **Figure 5**.
5. Enter a name for the bookmark and touch **Add** in the upper right-hand corner of the screen. The bookmark is added to the Home screen.

Figure 5: Add to Home Window

4. Managing Open Browser Windows

The Safari Web browser supports up to nine open browser windows. This feature is analogous to tabbed browsing in a browser like Mozilla Firefox or Google Chrome. Use the following tips when working with browser windows:

- To view the open Safari windows, touch the ⧉ button in the bottom right-hand corner of the screen in Safari. The open Safari windows appear, as shown in **Figure 6**. Touch the screen and flick your finger up or down to view other open windows.

- While viewing the open Safari windows, touch the ▣ button at the bottom left of the screen. A new browser window is opened.
- While viewing the open Safari windows, touch a window and move it to the left to close it. You can also touch **Done** to return to the window that you were just viewing.
- While viewing the open Safari windows, touch and hold a window and move it up or down to change its position in the list.

Figure 6: Open Safari Windows

5. Blocking Pop-Up Windows

Some websites may have pop-up windows that interfere with browsing the internet. To block pop-ups:

1. Touch the ⊙ icon on the Home screen. The Settings screen appears, as shown in **Figure 7**.
2. Scroll down and touch **Safari**. The Safari Settings screen appears, as shown in **Figure 8**.
3. Touch the ⬯ switch next to 'Block Pop-Ups'. Pop-ups will now be blocked.
4. Touch the ⬮ switch next to 'Block Pop-Ups'. Pop-ups will now be allowed.

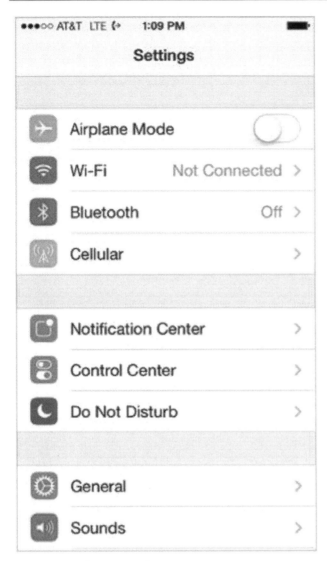

Figure 7: Settings Screen

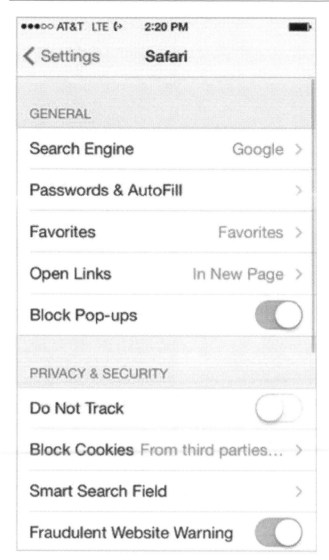

Figure 8: Safari Settings Screen

6. Changing the Search Engine

Google, Yahoo, or Bing can be set as the default search engine in Safari. When you get your new iPhone, the default search engine is set to Google. Touch the text field at the top right of the screen to use the search engine in Safari, as shown in **Figure 9**. To change the default search engine:

1. Touch the 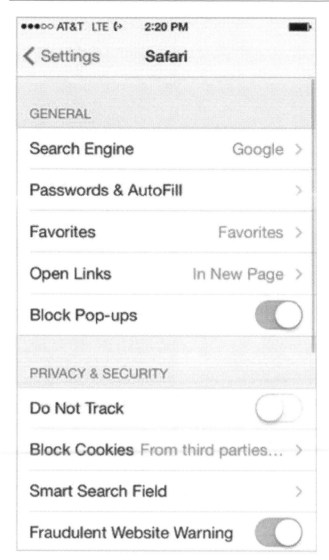 icon on the Home screen. The Settings screen appears.
2. Touch **Safari**. The Safari Settings screen appears.
3. Touch **Search Engine**. A list of search engines appears.

4. Touch the preferred search engine. The default search engine is set, and its name will now appear in the empty search field.

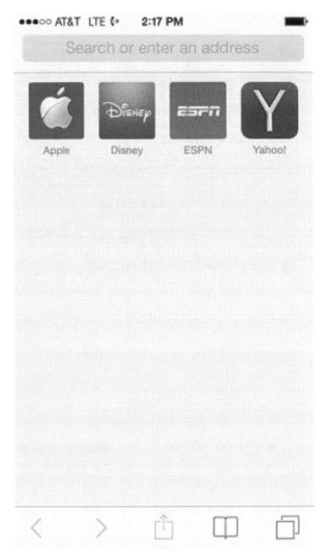

Figure 9: Search Field in Safari

7. Clearing the History, Cookies, and Cache

The iPhone can clear the list of recently visited websites, known as the History, as well as other data, such as saved passwords, known as Cookies. The iPhone can also delete data from previously visited websites, known as the Cache. To delete one or all of these items:

1. Touch the ⚙ icon on the Home screen. The Settings screen appears.
2. Touch **Safari**. The Safari Settings screen appears.
3. Touch **Clear History** or **Clear Cookies and Data**. A confirmation dialog appears.
4. Touch **Clear History** or **Clear Cookies and Data** again, depending on your selection in step 3. The selected data is deleted and the option is grayed out on the Safari Settings screen.

8. Viewing an Article in Reader Mode

The Safari browser can display certain news articles in Reader Mode, which allows you to read them like a book with no images or links. To view an article in Reader Mode, touch the ≡ button in the address bar at any time (when available), as outlined in **Figure 10**. Reader Mode turns on, as shown in **Figure 11**.

Figure 10: Reader Button in the Address Bar

Figure 11: Article in Reader Mode

9. Turning Private Browsing On or Off

In order to preserve privacy, the Safari Web browser allows you to surf the internet without saving the History or any other data showing that you have visited a particular website. To open a private window:

1. Touch the ⧉ button at the bottom of the Safari window. The open browser windows appear.
2. Touch **Private** at the bottom of the screen. A confirmation dialog appears.

3. Touch **Close All** to close the existing browser windows when the private browser window opens, or touch **Keep All** to leave them open. The Private Browser window opens.

10. Setting Up the AutoFill Feature

Safari can automatically fill in personal information, such as passwords and credit card information, to save you time when filling forms or shopping online. To set up the AutoFill feature:

1. Touch the ⚙ icon on the Home screen. The Settings screen appears.
2. Touch **Safari**. The Safari Settings screen appears.
3. Touch **Passwords & AutoFill**. The Passwords & Autofill screen appears, as shown in **Figure 12**.
4. Touch one of the following ⬭ switches turn on the corresponding AutoFill:

   - **Use Contact Info** - Enables the use of contact information when filling in forms. The Phonebook appears. Touch the name of a contact to use the contact information to fill in forms. It is recommended that you create a contact entry for yourself and use it for this feature.
   - **Names and Passwords** - Enables the use of saved names and passwords. You will be given the option to set up a security lock in order to keep your private information safe. Websites will give you the option to save your username and password. You can also touch the ⬭ switch next to 'Always Allow' to save passwords even for websites that will never save your password otherwise.
   - **Credit Cards** - Enables the use of saved credit card information. You will be given the option to set up a security lock in order to keep your private information safe. Touch **Saved Credit Cards**, and then touch **Add Credit Card** to add a new credit card.

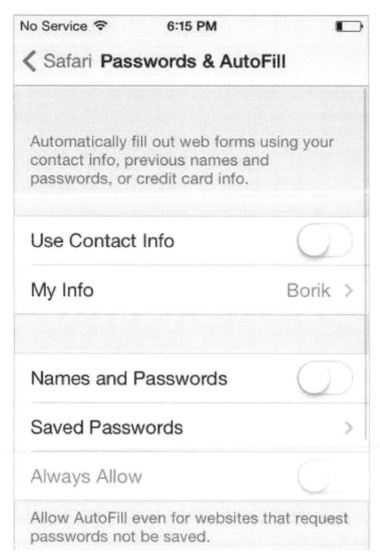

Figure 12: Passwords & Autofill Screen

11. Customizing the Smart Search Field

The address bar in the Safari browser can act as a search field that assists you by matching your search terms while you type. To customize the smart search field:

- Touch the ![icon] icon on the Home screen. The Settings screen appears.
- Touch **Safari**. The Safari Settings screen appears.
- Touch **Smart Search Field**. The Smart Search Field screen appears, as shown in **Figure 13**.

- Touch one of the following 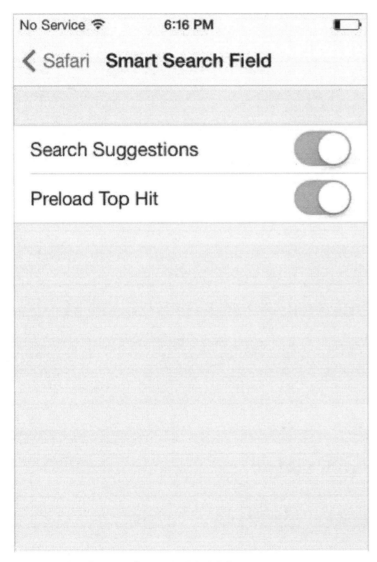 switches to turn on the corresponding smart search feature:

- **Search Suggestions** - Enables search term matching to assist you when performing a search.
- **Preload Top Hit** - Automatically loads the most popular search result when you perform a search. The web page is loaded in the background before you even touch the link.

Figure 13: Smart Search Field Screen

Managing Photos and Videos

Table of Contents

1. Taking a Picture

The iPhone 5S has a built-in eight-megapixel rear-facing camera and a 1.2 megapixel front-facing camera. To take a picture, touch the ![camera icon] icon. The camera turns on, as shown in **Figure 1**. Use the following tips when taking a picture:

- Touch the screen and slide your finger to the left to take a square picture. 'SQUARE' appears at the bottom of the screen. Touch the screen again and slide your finger to the right to activate the default camera. 'PHOTO' appears at the bottom of the screen.

- Touch the ![camera button] button in the upper right-hand corner of the screen at any time to use the front-facing camera.

- Touch the ![shutter button] button to take a picture. The shutter closes and opens, and the picture is automatically stored in the 'Camera Roll' album. If the surroundings are too dark, refer to *"Using the Flash"* on page 115 for help.

Note: Refer to "Tips and Tricks" *on page 294 to learn how to take a picture directly from the Lock screen.*

Figure 1: Camera Turned On

2. Capturing a Video

The iPhone has a built-in camcorder that can shoot HD video. To capture a video on the iPhone:

1. Touch the ![icon] icon. The camera turns on. The iPhone switches to Video Capture mode.

2. Touch the screen and slide your finger to the right. 'VIDEO' appears at the bottom of the screen, and the camcorder turns on.

3. Touch the ⬤ button. The camera begins to record.

4. Touch the ⬤ button. The camera stops recording and the video is automatically saved to the 'Moments' album.

Note: Touch the thumbnail in the bottom left-hand corner of the screen to preview the video.

3. Using the Digital Zoom

While taking pictures or capturing video, use the camera's built-in Digital Zoom feature if the subject of the photo is far away. Unfortunately, the Digital Zoom will not work when recording videos. To zoom in before taking a photo, touch the screen with two fingers and move them apart. The ▬━━━━○━━━━━━━━➕ appears at the bottom of the screen and the camera zooms in. To zoom out before taking a photo, touch the screen with two fingers apart and bring them together. The ▬━━○━━━━━━━━━➕ appears at the bottom of the screen and the camera zooms out.

Note: Because of its digital nature, the zoom function will not provide the best resolution, and the image may look fuzzy. It is recommended to be as close as possible to the subject of the photo.

4. Using the Flash

The iPhone has a built-in LED flash that can be used along with the rear-facing camera. When shooting a video with the flash turned on, it will remain on throughout the movie. To use the flash:

1. Make sure the camera is turned on and the rear camera is activated. Refer to *"Taking a Picture"* on page 113 to learn how.

2. Touch the ⚡ icon in the upper-left hand corner of the screen. The ⚡ Auto On Off menu appears.

3. Touch **On**. The flash is turned on and will be used when taking a picture or capturing a video.

4. Touch **Off.** The flash is turned off and will never be used.

5. Touch **Auto**. The flash will be used as needed, as determined by the iPhone's light sensor.

5. Focusing on a Part of the Screen

While taking pictures, the camera can focus on a particular object or area on the screen. This will adjust the lighting and other elements to make the object or area stand out in the picture. To focus on a specific part of the screen, just touch that area. An orange box appears and the camera focuses.

6. Browsing Photos

After taking pictures on your iPhone or transferring them from your computer, you may view them at any time. To view saved photos:

1. Touch the icon on the Home screen. The Photos application opens.
2. Touch **Albums** in the bottom right-hand corner of the screen. A list of photo albums appears, as shown in **Figure 2** . The photos you have taken with the iPhone are in an album called 'Camera Roll'.
3. Touch an album. The photos in the album appear.
4. Touch a photo. The photo appears in full screen.
5. Use the following tips when viewing photos:

   - Touch a photo with your thumb and forefinger and move the two fingers apart to zoom in on it. The zoom will center where your fingers were joined.
   - Touch the screen twice quickly to zoom out completely. Touch the photo with your thumb and forefinger spread apart and move the fingers together while touching the photo to zoom out gradually. Move your fingers apart to zoom in.
   - Touch the album name at the top left of the screen while viewing a photo to return to album view. If the album name is not shown, touch the photo once to make the photo menus appear at the top and bottom of the screen.

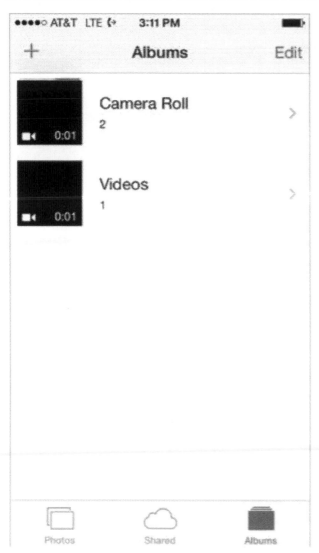

Figure 2: List of Photo Albums

7. Editing a Photo

The iPhone provides basic photo-editing tools. To edit a photo:

1. Touch the ✿ icon at the Home screen. The Photos application opens.
2. Touch **Albums** in the bottom right-hand corner of the screen. A list of photo albums appears.
3. Touch an album. The photos in the album appear.
4. Touch a photo. The photo appears in full screen.

5. Touch **Edit** in the upper right-hand corner of the screen. The Photo Editing menu appears at the bottom of the screen, as shown in **Figure 3**.
6. Touch one of the following icons to edit the photo:

- Rotates the photo 90 degrees counter-clockwise. Touch repeatedly to keep rotating the photo. Touch **Save** in the upper right-hand corner of the screen to save the changes.

- Enhances the quality of the photo. Touch **Save** in the upper right-hand corner of the screen to save the changes.

- Adds a color effect, such as mono (grayscale) or instant (Polaroid) to the photo.

- Removes red-eye from the photo. Touch each red eye in the photo and then touch **Apply** in the upper right-hand corner of the screen. Touch**Save** in the upper right-hand corner to save the changes.

- Crops the photo. Touch the corners of the photo and drag the selected portion, as shown in **Figure 4**. Touch **Constrain** at the bottom of the screen and touch a size to choose a custom crop, and then touch **Crop** in the upper right-hand corner of the screen. Touch **Save** in the upper right-hand corner to save the changes.

Figure 3: Photo Editing Menu

Figure 4: Cropping a Photo

8. Deleting a Photo

You may delete unwanted pictures from your iPhone to free up memory. To delete a photo:
Warning: Once a picture is deleted, there is no way to restore it. Deleting a picture removes it from all albums and Photo Stream.

1. Touch the [icon] icon. The Photos application opens.
2. Touch **Albums** in the bottom right-hand corner of the screen. A list of photo albums appears.
3. Touch an album. The photos contained in the album appear.
4. Touch a photo. The photo appears in full screen view.

5. Touch the 🗑 button in the bottom right-hand corner of the screen. A confirmation dialog appears.
6. Touch **Delete Photo**. The photo is deleted from all albums on the iPhone, as well as Photo Stream, if it was backed up.

9. Creating a Photo Album

You can create a photo album right on your iPhone. To create a photo album:

1. Touch the ✿ icon. The Photos application opens.
2. Touch **Albums** in the bottom right-hand corner of the screen. A list of photo albums appears.
3. Touch the ➕ button in the upper left-hand corner of the screen. The New Album window appears, as shown in **Figure 5**.
4. Enter a name for the album and touch **Save**. The new photo album is created and you can now choose photos to add to it.
5. Touch a photo album and then touch photos to add them. Touch a photo a second time to deselect it. Touch **Albums** in the bottom right-hand corner of the screen at any time to return to the album list.
6. Touch **Done** in the upper right-hand corner of the screen. The selected photos are added to the new photo album.

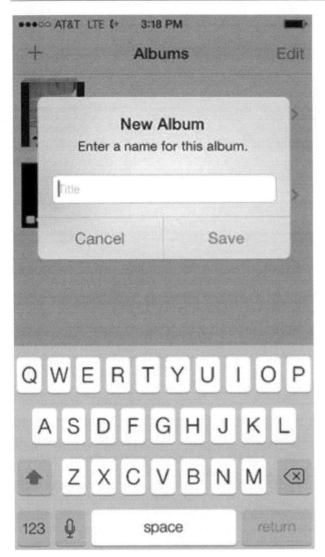

Figure 5: New Album Window

10. Editing a Photo Album

Photo albums stored on the iPhone can be edited right from your device. Refer to *"Creating a Photo Album"* on page 121 to learn how to make a new photo album using your phone.
To edit the name of a photo album:

1. Touch the 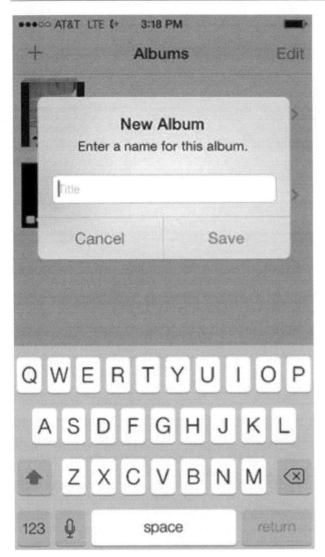 icon. The Photos application opens.
2. Touch **Albums** in the bottom right-hand corner of the screen. A list of photo albums appears.

3. Touch **Edit** in the upper right-hand corner of the screen. The ⊖ buttons appear to the left of the albums that may be edited.
4. Touch the name of a photo album. The virtual keyboard appears.
5. Enter a new name for the album and touch **Done** in the upper right-hand corner of the screen. The album is renamed.

To add photos to an album:

1. Touch the ✱ icon. The Photos application opens.
2. Touch **Albums** in the bottom right-hand corner of the screen. A list of photo albums appears.
3. Touch an album. The photos contained in the album appear.
4. Touch **Select** in the upper right-hand corner of the screen. Photos can now be selected.
5. Touch as many photos as desired. The photos are selected and ✓ icons appear on the thumbnails, as shown in **Figure 6**.
6. Touch **Add To** at the bottom of the screen. A list of photo albums appears. You cannot add the photos to any album that is grayed out.
7. Touch the name of a photo album. The selected photos are added to the album.

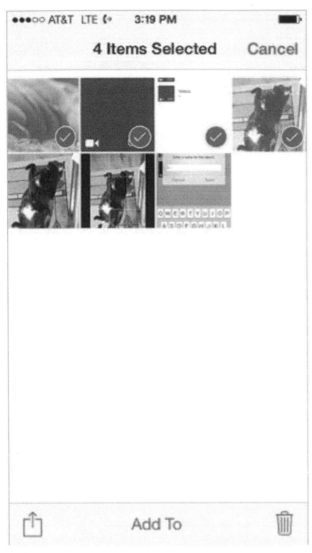

Figure 6: Selected Photos

11. Deleting a Photo Album

Photo albums stored on the iPhone can be deleted right from your phone. To delete a photo album:

Warning: When an album is deleted from the iPhone, any photos that are stored in other albums will remain on the iPhone. Make sure any photos you wish to keep are stored in another album. Refer to "Editing a Photo Album" on page 122 to learn how to add photos to an album.

1. Touch the icon. The Photos application opens.

2. Touch **Albums** in the bottom right-hand corner of the screen. A list of photo albums appears.

3. Touch **Edit** in the upper right-hand corner of the screen. The ⊖ buttons appear to the left of the albums that may be deleted.

4. Touch the ⊖ button next to an album. 'Delete' appears next to the album.
5. Touch **Delete**. A confirmation appears at the bottom of the screen.
6. Touch **Delete Album**. The photo album is deleted.

12. Starting a Slideshow

The iPhone can play a slideshow using the photos in your albums. To begin a slideshow:

1. Touch the 🌸 icon. The Photos application opens.
2. Touch **Albums** in the bottom right-hand corner of the screen. A list of photo albums appears.
3. Touch an album. The photos in the album appear.
4. Touch a photo. The photo appears in full screen.

5. Touch the ⬆ icon in the bottom left-hand corner of the screen. The Photo Selection screen appears.

6. Touch **Next** in the upper right-hand corner of the screen. The Photo Actions menu appears at the bottom of the screen, as shown in **Figure 7**.

7. Touch the ▷ button at the bottom of the screen. The Slideshow Settings screen appears, as shown in **Figure 8**.

8. Touch **Transitions** and select the transition for the slideshow. Touch the ⬯ switch to turn on Music from your library.

9. Touch **Start Slideshow** when ready. The slideshow begins.

Figure 7: Photo Actions Menu

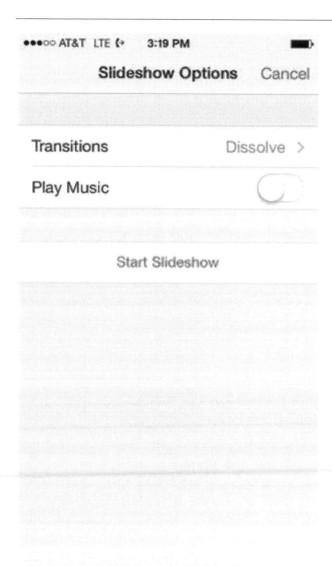

Figure 8: Slideshow Settings Screen

13. Saving a Picture from a Picture Message

After receiving a picture as an attachment in a text message, you may save it to a photo album. To save a picture from a picture message:

1. Touch the ⬤ icon. The Messages screen appears, as shown in **Figure 9**.
2. Touch the conversation that contains the picture. The Conversation screen appears.
3. Touch the photo in the conversation. The photo appears in full-screen view.
4. Touch the ⬆ icon. The Save Photo menu appears.
5. Touch **Save Image**. The photo is saved to the iPhone. By default, the photo is stored in the 'Camera Roll' album.

Figure 9: Messages Screen

14. Browsing Photos by Date and Location

The iPhone can sort photos according to the physical locations where they were taken, as well as the dates on which they were captured. To browse photos by date and location:

1. Touch the icon. The Photos application opens.
2. Touch **Collections** in the upper left-hand corner of the screen. A list of albums appears, organized by date and location, as shown in **Figure 10**.
3. Touch an album in any location. The selected album opens.
4. Touch the name of a town. A map appears, showing the locations where photos were taken, as shown in **Figure 11**. Touch **Collections** to return to the photo list.
5. Touch **Years** in the upper left-hand corner of the screen. A list of years when pictures were taken appears.

Figure 10: List of Albums Organized by Date and Location

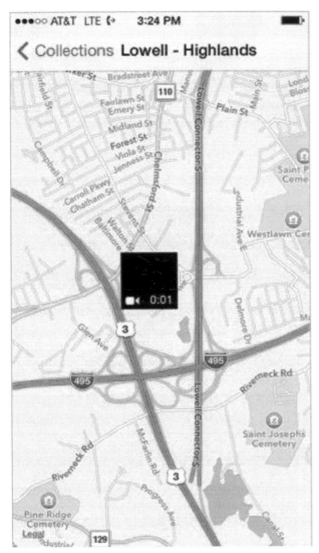

Figure 11: Photo Album Map

Using iTunes on the iPhone

Table of Contents

1. Setting Up an iTunes Account

In order to buy content, you will need to have an iTunes account. Refer to *"Setting Up an iTunes Account"* on page 181 to learn more.

2. Buying Music in iTunes

Music can be purchased directly from the iPhone via iTunes. To buy music using the iTunes application:

1. Touch the ![icon] icon. The iTunes application opens.

2. Touch the ♪ icon. The iTunes Music Store opens and the new releases are shown.

3. Touch **Featured**, **Charts**, or **Genres** at the top of the screen to browse music. The corresponding section appears.

4. Touch an album. The Album description appears, as shown in **Figure 1**.

5. Touch the price of the album. 'Buy Album' appears.

6. Touch **Buy Album**. The album is purchased. Touch the price of a song and then touch **Buy Song** to buy a single song.

7. Touch the ![icon] icon in the bottom right-hand corner of the screen, and then touch **Downloads** to view the download progress. The Downloads screen appears, as shown in **Figure 2**. If the list is empty, all downloads are complete.

Note: You may need to enter your iTunes password when purchasing music on the iPhone.

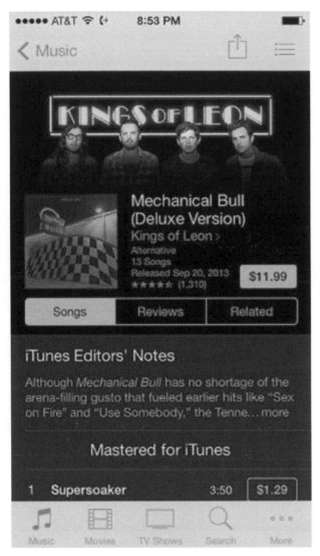

Figure 1: Album Description

Figure 2: Downloads Screen

3. Buying or Renting Videos in iTunes

Videos can be purchased or rented directly from the iPhone and viewed using the Music application. To buy videos using the iTunes application:

1. Touch the ![icon] icon. The iTunes application opens.
2. Touch the ![icon] icon or the ![icon] icon. The iTunes Video Store opens and the featured videos appear, as shown in **Figure 3** (Movie Store).

3. Touch **Featured**, **Charts**, or **Genres** at the top of the screen to browse videos. Touch a video. The Video description appears, as shown in **Figure 4**.
4. Touch the price of the video. 'Buy Movie', 'Rent Movie', or 'Buy HD Episode' appears, depending on your selection.
5. Touch **Buy ...**, where ... refers to the type of video that you are buying. The iPhone may ask for your iTunes password. The video is purchased or rented and the download begins.
6. Touch the ![icon] icon in the bottom right-hand corner of the screen, and then touch **Downloads** to view the download progress. The Downloads screen appears. If the list is empty, all downloads are complete.

Note: When renting a video, the video is available for 24 hours once you start watching it. Once 24 hours has passed, you will not be able to resume the video if you pause it.

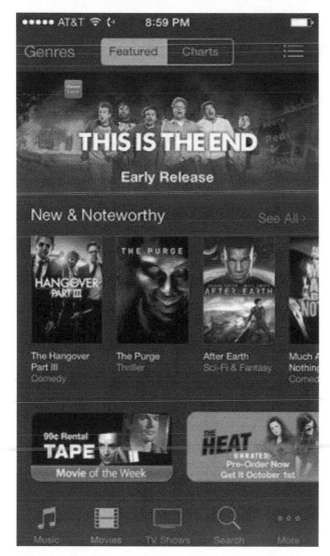

Figure 3: iTunes Video Store (Movies)

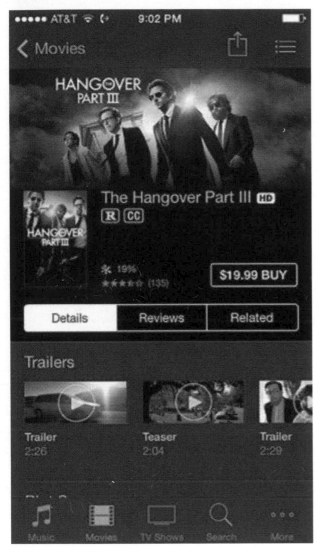

Figure 4: Video Description

4. Buying Tones in iTunes

Ringtones can be purchased directly from your iPhone to use for incoming calls. To buy ringtones using the iTunes application:

1. Touch the ![icon] icon. The iTunes application opens.
2. Touch the ![icon] icon in the bottom right-hand corner of the screen. The More screen appears, as shown in **Figure 5**.
3. Touch **Tones**. The iTunes Tones Store opens, as shown in **Figure 6**.

4. Touch **Genres** or **Tones** at the top of the screen to browse ringtones. Touch a ringtone. A preview of the ringtone plays.
5. Touch the price of the ringtone. 'BUY TONE' appears.
6. Touch **BUY TONE**. The ringtone is purchased and downloaded to the iPhone.
7. Touch the ⊙ ⊙ ⊙ icon in the bottom right-hand corner of the screen, and then touch **Downloads** to view the download progress. The Downloads screen appears. If the list is empty, all downloads are complete.

To set the new ringtone as the default:

1. Touch the ⊚ icon on the Home screen. The Settings screen appears, as shown in **Figure 7**.
2. Touch **Sounds**. The Sound Settings screen appears, as shown in **Figure 8**.
3. Touch **Ringtone**. A list of ringtones appears.
4. Touch the recently downloaded ringtone. The ringtone is set as the default.

Note: Refer to "Assigning a Custom Ringtone to a Contact" *on page 300 to learn how to assign the new ringtone to a specific contact.*

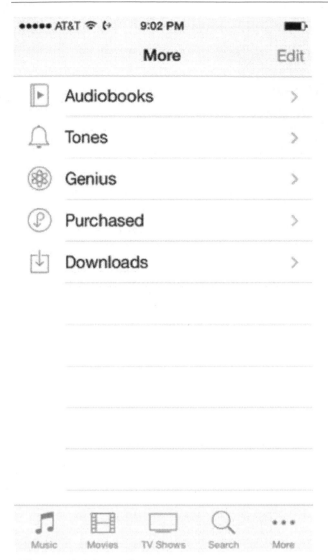

Figure 5: More Screen

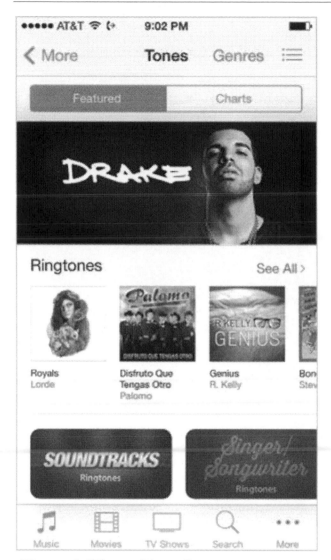

Figure 6: iTunes Tone Store

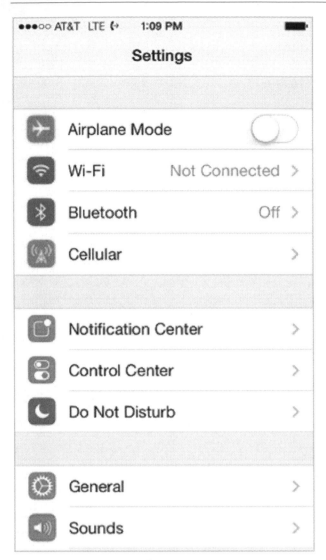

Figure 7: Settings Screen

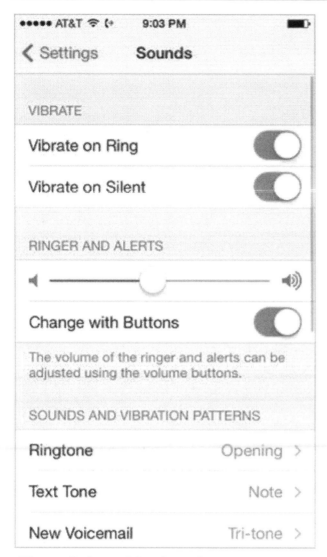

Figure 8: Sound Settings Screen

5. Searching for Media in iTunes

The iPhone can search for any media in the iTunes Store. To search for media:

1. Touch the icon. The iTunes application opens.

2. Touch the icon. The search field appears at the top of the screen. Touch the search field. Touch the button to clear the field, if necessary.

3. Enter the name of a song, video, or ringtone you wish to find. Touch **Search** in the lower right-hand corner of the screen. The matching results appear, organized by the type of media, as shown in **Figure 9**.
4. Touch a song, video, or ringtone. The media description appears.

Note: Refer to "Buying Music in iTunes" *on page 133*, "Buying or Renting Videos in iTunes" *on page 136, or* "Buying Tones in iTunes" *on page 138 to learn how to purchase media.*

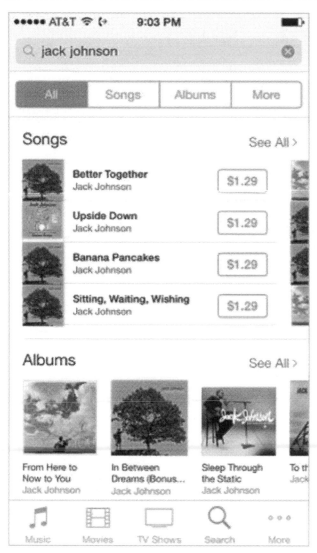

Figure 9: Available Media Results

6. Playing Media

To play media purchased in iTunes on the iPhone, use the Music application. Refer to *"Using the Music Application"* on page 146 to learn how to use the Music application.

Using the Music Application

Table of Contents

1. Downloading Media

Use the iTunes Application to download media to the iPhone. Refer to *"Using iTunes on the iPhone"* to learn how.

2. Playing Music

The Music application on the iPhone can be used to play music. To listen to your music:

1. Touch the icon. The Music application opens.
2. Touch one of the following icons at the bottom of the screen to browse music:

 - Browse existing playlists.

 - Browse existing artists.

 - Browse existing songs.

○ ○ ○ - Browse existing albums, genres, compilations, or composers.

3. Use the following tips to navigate the Music Application:

   • Touch a playlist, artist, or song to play the item. The item plays, as shown in **Figure 1**.
   • Tilt the iPhone horizontally. The album art for the available albums appears, as shown in **Figure 2**.

- After you have exited the Music application, touch the screen at the bottom and drag your finger up to bring up the music controls. Touch the name of the artist to return to the Music application. The music controls will also appear on the lock screen.

Figure 1: Music Playing

Figure 2: Album View

Figure 3: Music Controls

Figure 4: Music Controls on the Lock Screen

3. Using Additional Audio Controls

Use the Song Controls to control music while it is playing. Touch one of the following to perform the corresponding function:

◀◀ - Skip to the beginning of the current song or skip to the previous song.

▶▶ - Skip to the next song.

❚❚ - Pause the current song.

▶ - Resume the current song when it is paused.

≡ - View the current playlist.

- **Repeat** - Repeat the song or artist that is currently playing.

▬▬▬|▬▬▬▬▬▬▬▬▬▬▬▬▬▬ - Drag the | on the bar at the top of the screen to go to a different part of the song.
  - **Shuffle** - Shuffle all songs in the playlist. Touch again to play the songs in order.
  - **Create** - Create an iTunes Radio station from the artist or song that is currently playing.

Note: Touch both **Repeat** *and* **Shuffle** *to play songs continuously in random order. To shuffle and play all songs on the iPhone, go to the song list and touch* **Shuffle**.

4. Creating a Playlist

Playlists can be created in iTunes. However, the Music application can perform the same function. To create a playlist in the Music application:

1. Touch the 🎵 icon in the Music application. The existing playlists appear.
2. Touch **New Playlist**. The New Playlist window appears, as shown in **Figure 5** .
3. Enter the name of the playlist and touch **Save**. A list of the songs on your iPhone appears, as shown in **Figure 6**.
4. Touch one of the icons at the bottom of the screen to browse music to add to the new playlist. Refer to *"Playing Music"* on page 146 to learn more about finding music in the Music application.
5. Touch a song. The song is grayed out and added to the playlist.
6. Touch **Done** in the upper right-hand corner of the screen. The playlist is populated with the selected music.

After creating a playlist, you can add or remove music from it. To edit a playlist:

1. Touch the 🎵 icon in the Music application. The available playlists appear.
2. Touch a playlist. The Playlist screen appears, as shown in **Figure 7**.

3. Touch **Edit**. A ⊖ button appears next to every song in the playlist.

4. Touch the ⊖ button next to a song. The song is removed from the playlist.

5. Touch the ╬ button in the upper right-hand corner of the screen to add songs. To add songs, repeat steps 4 and 5 from the instructions above. The selected songs are added to the playlist.

6. Touch **Done**. The changes to the playlist are saved.

Note: Removing a song from a playlist will not delete it from the Music library.

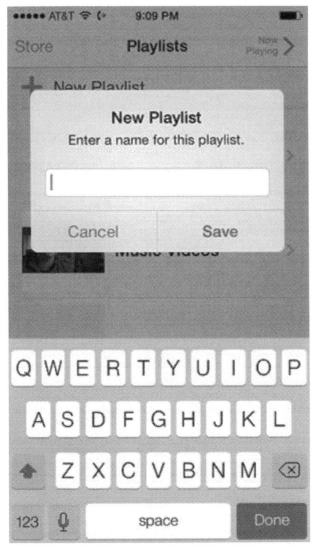

Figure 5: New Playlist Window

Figure 6: List of Songs on Your iPhone

Figure 7: Playlist Screen

5. Using the iTunes Radio

iOS 7 introduced the iTunes Radio, which is a free service that allows you to create personalized stations based on artists, songs, or genres.

To create a new iTunes Radio station:

1. Touch the ⬜ icon in the Music application. The iTunes Radio screen appears, as shown in **Figure 9**.

2. Touch the ✚ icon. The New Station screen appears, as shown in **Figure 10**.
3. Touch a genre in the list, or touch the search field at the top of the screen, and enter an artist, genre, or song. A preview of the station begins to play.

4. Touch the ⊕ icon next to the station name. The station is added to your stations.

Figure 8: iTunes Radio Screen

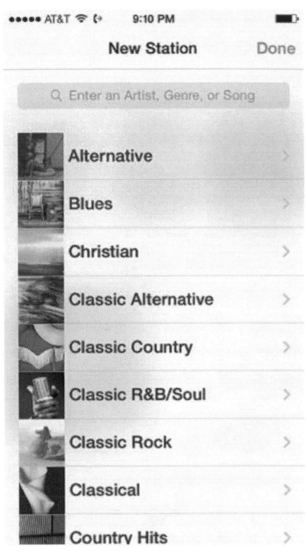

Figure 9: New Station Screen

6. Tips and Shortcuts

Refer to *"Music Tips and Tricks"* starting on page 299 to learn how to change the navigation icons in the Music application, delete music right from your iPhone, and more.

Using the Email Application

Table of Contents

1. Setting Up the Email Application

Before the Email application can be used, at least one account must be set up on your iPhone. To set up the Email application:

1. Touch the icon. The Settings screen appears, as shown in **Figure 1**.
2. Scroll down and touch **Mail, Contacts, Calendars**. The Mail, Contacts, Calendars screen appears, as shown in **Figure 2**.
3. Touch **Add Account**. The Account Type screen appears, as shown in **Figure 3**.
4. Touch one of the email services in the list to set up an email account. The corresponding email setup screen appears.
5. Enter all of the required information and touch **Next** in the upper right-hand corner of the screen. The email account is added to your iPhone.

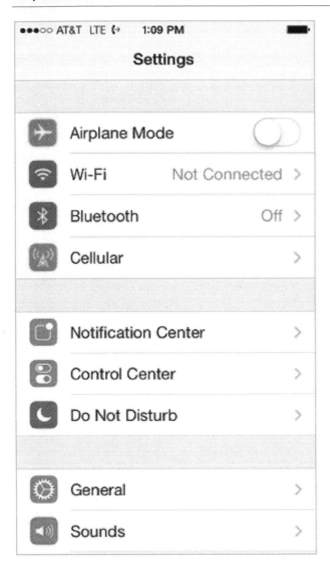

Figure 1: Settings Screen

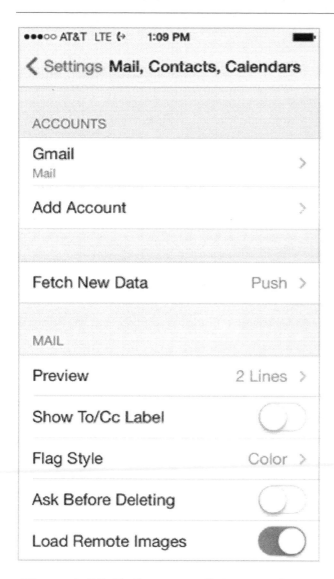

Figure 2: Mail, Contacts, Calendars Screen

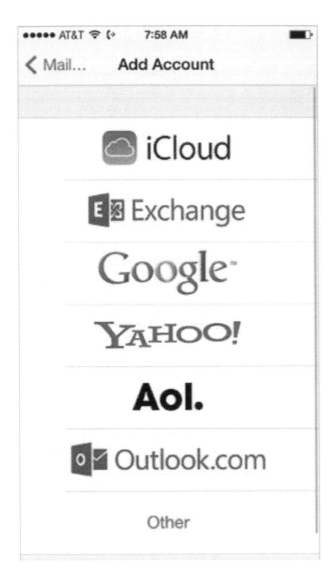

Figure 3: Account Type Screen

2. Reading Email

You can read your email on the iPhone via the Email application. Before opening the Email application, make sure you have set up your email account. Refer to *"Setting Up the Email Application"* on page 157 to learn how. To read your email:

1. Touch the 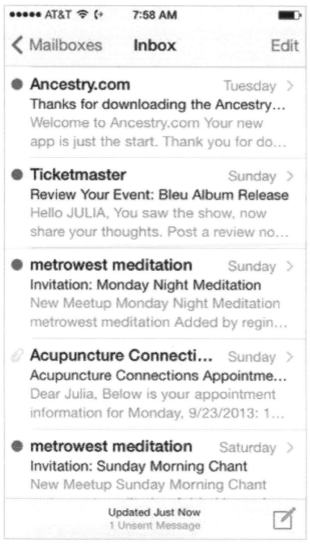 icon. The Email application opens and the Inbox appears, as shown in **Figure 4**. If the emails are not shown, touch **Inbox** in the upper left-hand corner of the screen if the name of your email is shown. This is the same name you gave the account when setting it up.
2. Touch an email. The email opens.
3. Touch **Inbox** in the upper left-hand corner of the screen in an email to return to the list of received emails. Touch **Mailboxes** in the upper left-hand corner of the Inbox to return to the list of mailboxes. The mailbox list varies depending on the mail service.

Figure 4: Email Inbox

3. Switching Accounts in the Email Application

If you have more than one active email account, you can switch between them or view all of your email in one Inbox. To switch to another account:

1. Touch the icon. The Email application opens and your emails appear.
2. Touch **Mailboxes** in the upper left-hand corner of the screen while viewing a list of messages in a folder. A list of all active inboxes and accounts appears, as shown in **Figure 5**.
3. Touch an account. The Inbox associated with the selected account appear.

Note: You can also touch **All Inboxes** *to view all emails from the accounts attached to your iPhone in a single joint folder.*

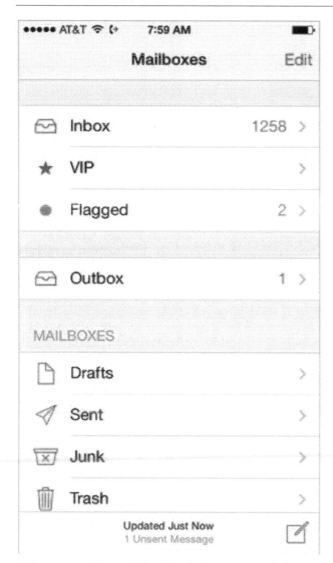

Figure 5: List of Active Inboxes and Accounts

4. Writing an Email

Compose email directly from the iPhone using the Email application. To write an email while using the Email application:

1. Touch the ✎ button in the bottom right-hand corner of the screen. The New Email screen appears, as shown in **Figure 6**.
2. Start entering the name of a contact. A list of matching contacts appears below as you type.
3. Touch the name of the contact that you wish to email. The contact's email address is added to the addressee list. Alternately, enter an email address from scratch. Enter as many additional addressees as desired.
4. Touch the text field to the right of 'Subject' and enter a topic for the message. The subject is entered.
5. Touch **return** in the bottom right-hand corner of the keyboard. The cursor jumps to the body of the email.
6. Enter the content of the email and touch **Send** in the upper right-hand corner of the screen. The email is sent.

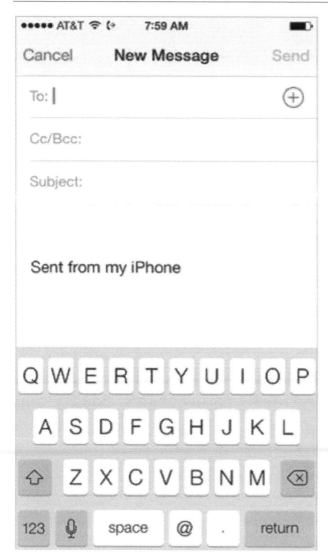

Figure 6: New Email Screen

5. Formatting Text

When writing an email on your iPhone, you can format the text to add bold, italics, underline, or increase the quote level.

To add bold, italics, or underline text while writing an email:

1. Touch and hold the text in the email that you wish to format. The Select menu appears above the text, as shown in **Figure 7**.

2. Touch **Select All**. All of the text is selected. To select a single word, touch **Select**. Blue dots appear around the word or phrase.

3. Touch and hold one of the blue dots and drag it in any direction. The text between the dots is highlighted and a Text menu appears, as shown in **Figure 8**.

4. Touch the button. 'Bold', 'Italics', and 'Underline' appear. If you do not see button, touch the button in the Text menu.

5. Touch one of the formatting options. The associated formatting is applied to the selected text.

You can also increase the left margin, or quote level, in an email. To increase the quote level:

1. Touch and hold any location in your email. The text cursor flashes in the selected location.

2. Touch the button in the Text menu. The Text Format menu appears.

3. Touch **Quote Level**. The Quote Level options appear.

4. Touch **Decrease** or **Increase** to adjust the Quote Level accordingly. The new Quote Level is set and applied to the paragraph where the text cursor is currently flashing.

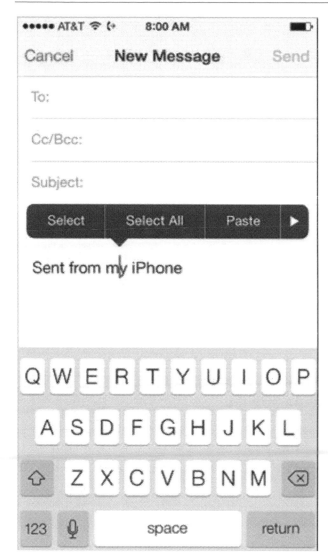

Figure 7: Select Menu

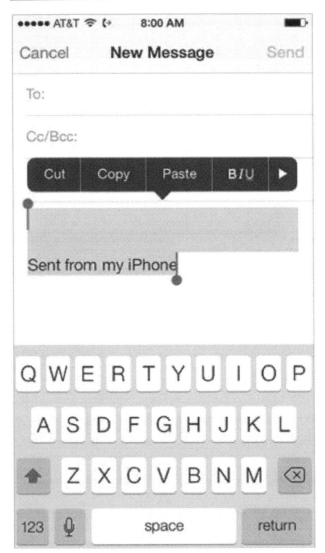

Figure 8: Text Menu

6. Replying to and Forwarding Email Messages

After receiving an email, you can reply to the sender or forward the email to a new recipient. To reply to, or forward, an email message:

1. Touch the ✉ icon. The Email application opens.
2. Touch an email. The email appears.
3. Touch the ↩ button at the bottom of the screen. The Reply menu appears, as shown in **Figure 9**.

4. Touch **Reply** to reply to the message or touch **Forward** to forward the message. The New Message screen appears. The subject at the top is preceded by 'Re:' if replying or 'Fwd:' if forwarding. The original email is copied in the body. If replying, the addressee field is filled in.
5. Touch the text field next to 'To:' and enter an addressee, if necessary. The addressee is entered.
6. Touch the text field to the right of 'Subject' to enter a different subject for your message, if desired. The subject is entered.
7. Touch the text field below 'Subject' and enter a message, if desired. The message is entered.
8. Touch **Send** in the upper right-hand corner of the screen. The email is sent.

Note: When forwarding, the attachment menu will appear if the original message has an attachment. Touch **Include** *if you wish to include the attachment when you forward the email. Otherwise, touch* **Don't Include**.

Figure 9: Reply Menu

7. Attaching a Picture or Video to an Email

While composing an email, you may wish to attach a picture or video to send to the recipient. To attach a picture or video to an email:

1. Touch and hold anywhere in the content of the email. The Select menu appears above the text.

2. Touch the ▶ button in the Select menu, and then touch **Insert Photo or Video**. A list of photo albums stored on your iPhone appears, as shown in **Figure 10**.

3. Touch the photo album that contains the photo that you wish to attach. The photo album opens and a list of photo thumbnails appears, as shown in **Figure 11**.
4. Touch the photo that you wish to attach. A preview of the photo appears.
5. Touch **Choose**. The selected photo is attached. Alternatively, touch **Cancel** to return to the list of photos.

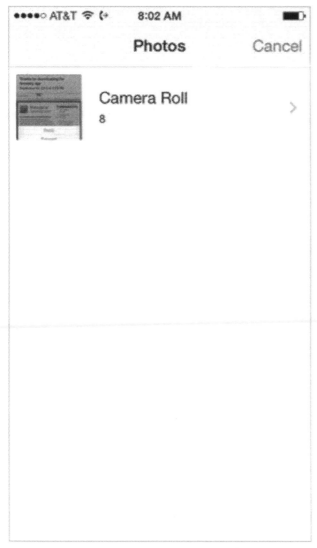

Figure 10: List of Photo Albums

Figure 11: List of Photo Thumbnails

8. Moving an Email in the Inbox to Another Folder

You may wish to organize emails into folders so that you can find them more easily. To move an email in the Inbox to another folder:

1. Touch an email in the Inbox. The email opens.

2. Touch the ⬜ button at the bottom of the screen. A list of available folders appears, as shown in **Figure 12**.

3. Touch the name of a folder. The selected email is moved to the folder. To view a list of your folders, touch **Mailboxes** in the upper left-hand corner of the screen while viewing the Inbox.

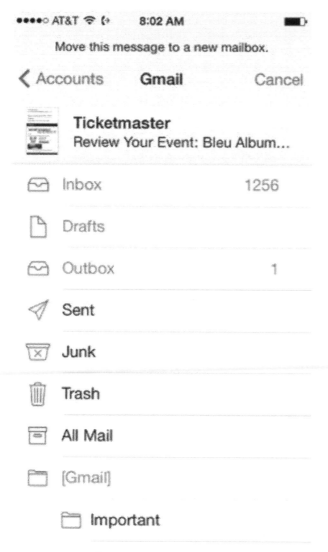

Figure 12: List of Available Folders

9. Flagging an Important Email

You may flag emails that are of the greatest importance in order to find them more quickly. This feature is especially useful if you do not have the time to read the email immediately, and wish to return to it in the near future. To flag an important email:

1. Touch an email in the Inbox. The email opens.

2. Touch the ⚑ button at the bottom of the screen. The Flagging menu appears, as shown in **Figure 13**.

3. Touch **Flag**. The email is flagged as 'Important'. You may also touch **Mark as Unread** to flag the email so that you remember to read it later.

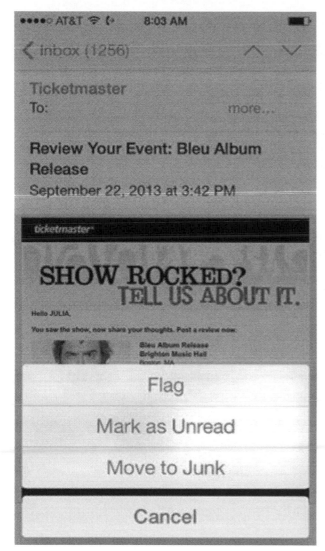

Figure 13: Flagging Menu

10. Archiving Emails

You may archive emails from your Inbox to free up space and improve organization. Archiving emails moves them to a folder that does not take up space on your phone. Therefore, you never need to delete an email, and can always recover it if you did not mean to delete it. You may archive as many emails as you like. To archive an email:

1. Touch the icon. The email application opens.
2. Touch and hold an email in the list and drag your finger to the left. 'Archive' appears to the right of the email.

3. Touch **Archive**. The email is sent to the Archive folder and disappears from the Inbox.

You can also archive an email by touching the ▢ icon at the bottom of the screen while viewing an open email.

*Note: Touch **Mailboxes** in the upper left-hand corner of the screen and then touch **All Mail** to view all emails, including those that have been archived.*

11. Changing the Default Signature

The iPhone can set a default signature that will be attached to the end of each email that is sent from the phone. To set or change this signature:

1. Touch the ⊚ icon. The Settings screen appears.
2. Touch **Mail, Contacts, Calendars** at the bottom of the screen. The Mail, Contacts, Calendars screen appears.
3. Scroll down and touch **Signature**. The Signature screen appears, as shown in **Figure 14**.
4. Enter a signature and touch **Mail...** in the upper left-hand corner of the screen when finished. The new signature is saved.

Figure 14: Signature Screen

12. Changing How You Receive Email

There are two options for receiving email on the iPhone. The iPhone can check for new email only when you refresh the Inbox, or it can constantly check for email and display an alert when a new email arrives. To set the iPhone to either check for email at regular intervals or only when you refresh the Inbox:

1. Touch the  icon. The Settings screen appears.
2. Touch **Mail, Contacts, Calendars** at the bottom of the screen. The Mail, Contacts, Calendars screen appears.

3. Touch **Fetch New Data**. The Fetch New Data screen appears, as shown in **Figure 15**.

4. Touch the ⬭ switch next to 'Push'. Push is turned on, and the Email application will constantly check for new email and alert you when a new one arrives.

5. Touch the ⬤ switch next to 'Push'. Push is turned off, and the Email application will only check for new email when you touch the top of the Inbox and slide your finger down to refresh it.

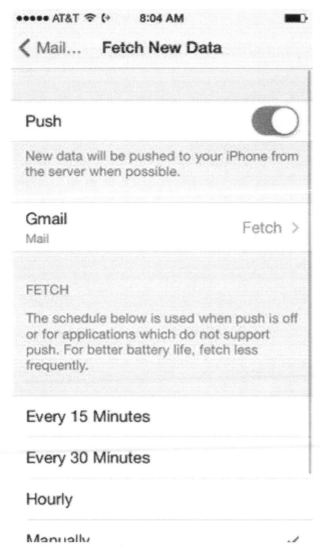

Figure 15: Fetch New Data Screen

13. Changing Email Options

There are various options that change the way your Email application works. Touch the ⚙ icon and then touch **Mail, Contacts, Calendars** to change one of the following options:

- **Preview** - Choose the number of lines of an email message to preview in the Inbox.
- **Show To/Cc Label** - Choose whether to hide the 'To' and 'Cc' labels and show only addresses.

- **Flag Style** - Choose the type of shape to use (color or shape) when flagging an email.
- **Ask Before Deleting** - Choose whether to display a confirmation before deleting an email.
- **Load Remote Images** - Choose whether to load images in an email automatically.
- **Organize by Thread** - Choose whether to group all emails with the same contact as a conversation.
- **Always Bcc Myself** - Choose whether the email application sends a copy of each email to your own email address for your records.
- **Increase Quote Level** - Choose whether to increase the left margin when replying to or forwarding an email.

Managing Applications

Table of Contents

1. Setting Up an iTunes Account

In order to buy applications, you will need to have an iTunes account. To set up a new iTunes account:

1. Touch the ⬤ icon. The Settings screen appears, as shown in **Figure 1**.
2. Scroll down and touch **iTunes & App Store**. The iTunes & App Store Settings screen appears, as shown in **Figure 2**. If you already have an Apple ID, enter your Apple ID and password and touch **Sign In**. Otherwise, proceed to step 3.
3. Touch **Create New Apple ID**. The New Account screen appears, as shown in **Figure 3**.
4. Touch the country where you live and touch **Done**. The country is selected.
5. Touch **Next** in the lower right-hand corner of the screen. The iTunes agreement screen appears.
6. Read the agreement and touch **Agree**. An acknowledgement dialog appears.
7. Touch **Agree**. The Account screen appears.

8. Touch each field and enter the required information. Touch **Next** in the bottom right-hand corner of the screen. The next Account Creation screen appears.
9. Touch each field and enter your credit card information. Touch **Next**. Your account is created.

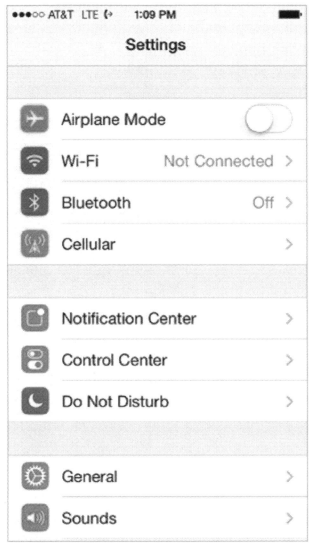

Figure 1: Settings Screen

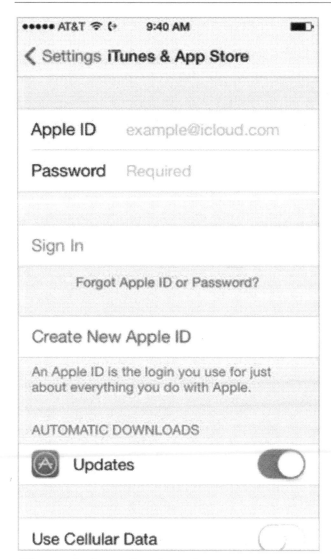

Figure 2: Store Settings Screen

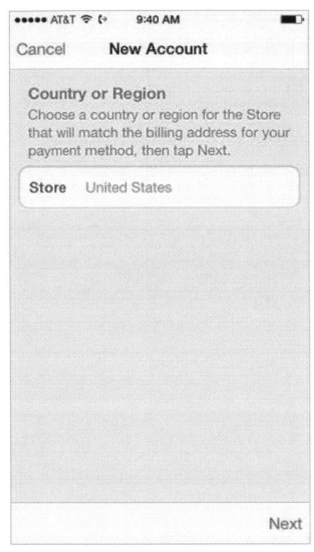

Figure 3: New Account Screen

2. Signing In to a Different iTunes Account

If more than one person uses your iPhone, you may wish to sign in with an alternate Apple ID. Only one Apple ID may be signed in at a time. To sign out and sign in to a different iTunes account:

1. Touch the ![icon] icon. The Settings screen appears.
2. Scroll down and touch **iTunes & App Store**. The iTunes & App Store Settings screen appears. If someone is signed in to their iTunes account on the iPhone, their email appears at the top of the screen.
3. Touch the email address at the top of the screen. The Apple ID window appears, as shown in **Figure 4**.
4. Touch **Sign Out**. The account is signed out.
5. Touch **Apple ID**. The virtual keyboard appears.
6. Enter your registered email address and password. Refer to *"Setting Up an iTunes Account"* on page 181 to learn how to create a new iTunes account.
7. Touch **Sign In**. The account is signed in and the owner's email is shown at the top of the iTunes & App Store screen.

Figure 4: Apple ID Window

3. Editing iTunes Account Information

You must keep your account information up to date in order to purchase applications from the iTunes Application Store. For instance, when your billing address changes or your credit card expires, you must change your information. To edit iTunes account information:

1. Touch the ![icon] icon. The Settings screen appears.
2. Scroll down and touch **iTunes & App Store**. The iTunes & App Store Settings screen appears. If someone is signed in to their iTunes account on the iPhone, their email appears at the top of the screen.

3. Touch **Sign In** and **Use Existing Apple ID** if you are not signed in. Enter your registered email and password and touch **OK**. You are signed in.
4. Touch your email at the top of the screen. The Apple ID window appears.
5. Touch **View Apple ID**. The Account Screen appears with your personal account information.
6. Touch a field to edit it, and then touch **Done** in the upper right-hand corner of the screen. The new information is saved.

4. Searching for an Application to Purchase

Use the Application Store to search for applications. There are three ways to search for applications:

Manual Search

To search for an application manually:

1. Touch the ![icon] icon. The Application Store opens, as shown in **Figure 5**.
2. Touch the ![magnifier] button at the bottom of the screen. The Search field appears at the top of the screen, as shown in **Figure 6**.
3. Touch **Search** at the top of the screen. The virtual keyboard appears at the bottom of the screen.
4. Enter the name of an application and touch **Search** in the lower right-hand corner of the screen. A list of matching results appears.

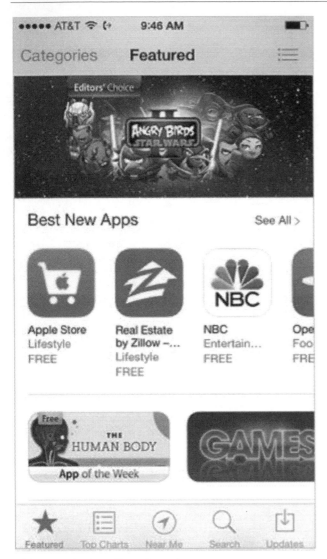

Figure 5: Application Store

Figure 6: Search Field in the Application Store

Browse by Category

To browse applications by category:

1. Touch the icon. The Application Store opens.
2. Touch Categories in the upper left-hand corner of the screen. The Categories screen appears, as shown in **Figure 7**. Touch the screen and move your finger up or down to scroll through the categories.
3. Touch a category to browse it. Some categories have sub-categories. Repeat step 2 to find the sub-category that you need.

Figure 7: Categories Screen

Browse by Popularity

To browse applications by popularity:

1. Touch the icon. The Application Store opens.
2. Touch the icon at the bottom of the screen. The Top Charts screen appears, as shown in **Figure 8** .
3. Touch one of the following to browse applications:
   - **Paid** - View the most popular paid applications.
   - **Free** - View the most popular free applications.
   - **Top Grossing** - View the most popular applications that have earned their creators the most money.

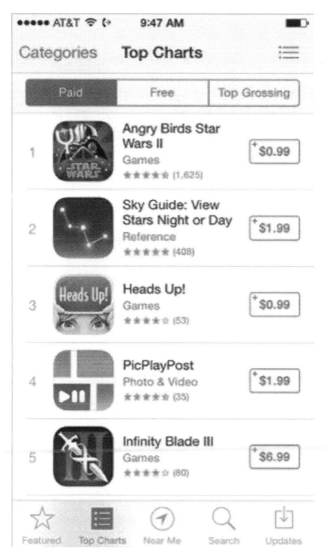

Figure 8: Top Charts Screen

5. Buying an Application

You may purchase applications directly from your iPhone. To buy an application:

1. Touch the ![app store icon] icon. The Application Store opens.
2. Find an application. Refer to *"Searching for an Application to Purchase"* on page 187 to learn how.
3. Touch an application in the list. The Application description appears, as shown in **Figure 9**.

4. Touch the price of the application or the word **FREE** next to the name of the application. 'BUY' appears if the application is paid or 'INSTALL' if the application is free. If the application is already downloaded to your iPhone, 'INSTALLED' appears.
   Touch **BUY** or **INSTALL**. The password prompt appears.

5. Enter your iTunes password and touch **OK**. The iPhone returns to the Home screen and the application is downloaded and installed.

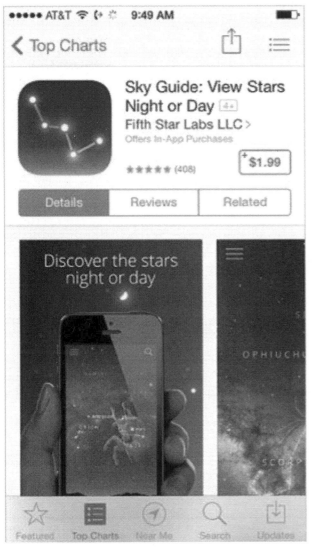

Figure 9: Application Description

6. Using iTunes to Download an Application from a Computer

You may also use iTunes on your computer to purchase and download applications for your iPhone in case your iPhone is not accessible. To use iTunes to purchase and download applications from your computer:

1. Install iTunes. Go to **www.itunes.com/download** to download it. Click **Download Now** and follow the on-screen instructions. iTunes downloads and installs.
2. Open iTunes and connect the iPhone to your computer using the provided USB cable. This is the same cable used to charge your iPhone. Unplug the USB end from the power adapter and plug that end into a USB port on your computer. Make sure the iPhone is on. 'Sync in Progress' appears on the iPhone.
3. The first time the iPhone is connected, iTunes will ask you to register. You can do this later. Just click **Register Later** or **Never Register** to ignore this.
4. Click **iTunes Store** in the upper right-hand corner of the screen. The iTunes store opens, as shown in **Figure 10**.
5. Click **App Store** at the top of the page. The Application Store opens.
6. Click **Search Store** in the upper right-hand corner of the screen and type in an application name or keyword. Available results appear.
7. Click the name of an application. The Application description appears, as shown in **Figure 11**.
8. Click **Buy App**. The iTunes Sign In dialog appears.
9. Type in your registered email address and password and click **Buy**. A confirmation dialog appears.
10. Click **Buy**. The application is purchased.
11. Click **iPhone** under 'Devices' when the download is finished. The iPhone summary screen appears.
12. Click **Sync** in the bottom right-hand corner of the screen. The iPhone lights up and "Sync in Progress" appears at the top of the screen. The current task is displayed at the top of the screen. When "OK to disconnect" appears at the top of the screen, your new application is installed and you may unplug the iPhone from your computer.

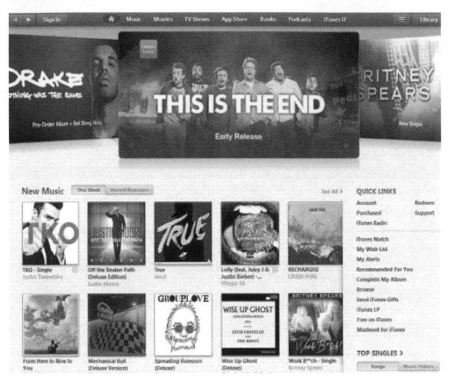

Figure 10: iTunes Store on a Computer

Figure 11: Application Description

7. Using Wi-Fi to Download an Application

Applications that are over 10MB in size require the iPhone to be connected to a Wi-Fi network to download. These applications will display the following message: "Application over 10MB. Connect to a Wi-Fi network or use iTunes on your computer to download >APP NAME<''', where APP NAME refers to the name of the application you are trying to download. Refer to *"Using Wi-Fi"* ion page 24 to learn how to turn on Wi-Fi or to *"Using iTunes to Download an Application from a Computer"* on page 193 to learn how to use iTunes on your computer.

8. Switching Between Applications

The iPhone allows you to switch between running applications without having to exit any of them. For instance, you can listen to Pandora radio and read an eBook at the same time. To switch between applications:

1. Touch an application icon on one of your Home screens. The application opens.
2. Press the **Home** button. The Home screen is shown.
3. Open another application. Press the **Home** button twice quickly. All of the open applications are displayed, as shown in **Figure 12**.
4. Touch an application icon. The iPhone switches to the selected application.

Note: When switching to another application, the first application is never automatically closed. The application is simply running in the background. Refer to "Closing an Application Running in the Background" *on page 196 to learn how to close an application.*

Figure 12: Open Applications

9. Closing an Application Running in the Background

After pressing the Home button to exit an application, it is not closed, but is left running in the background instead. It is good to have the application running, because you can always switch to it quickly. However, if an application stops responding or if your battery is dying too quickly, you may wish to close it. To close an application running in the background, press the **Home** button twice quickly. All of the open applications are displayed. Touch and hold an application icon and slide your finger up. The application is closed. You can also close multiple applications at the same time by touching two or more applications and sliding your fingers up. Switch to an open application by touching it in the list.

10. Organizing Applications into Folders

To learn how to organize applications into folders, click *"Creating an Icon Folder"* on page 23.

11. Reading User Reviews

In order to make a more informed decision when purchasing an application, you can read the reviews written by other users. However, be aware that people who have not used the application can also post reviews, which are uninformed. To read user reviews for an application:

1. Touch the   icon. The Application Store opens.
2. Find the application you want. Refer to *"Searching for an Application to Purchase"* on page 187 to learn how.
3. Touch an application icon. The Application description appears.
4. Touch the **Reviews** below the name of the application. The reviews for the application appear.

12. Changing Application Settings

Some applications have settings that can be changed from the Settings screen. To change the

Application settings, touch the   icon. The Settings screen appears. Touch an application below 'Game Center' at the bottom of the screen. The Application Settings screen appears. The settings on this screen depend on the particular application.

13. Deleting an Application

You may delete most applications from your iPhone to free up space on your memory card or Home screen. To delete an unwanted application:

1. Touch and hold an application icon. All of the applications on the Home screen begin to

   shake. Applications that can be erased have an   button in their top left corner.

2. Touch the   button next to an application icon. A confirmation dialog appears.
3. Touch **Delete**. The application is deleted.

4. Press the **Home** button. The application icons stop shaking and the buttons disappear.

Note: If you delete a paid application, you can download it again free of charge at any time. Refer to "Buying an Application" *on page 191 and follow the instructions for buying the application to re-download it.*

14. Sending an Application as a Gift

On the iPhone 5S, applications can be sent as gifts directly to someone's email. To send an application as a gift:

1. Touch the icon. The Application Store opens.
2. Find the application that you want to give as a gift. Refer to *"Searching for an Application to Purchase"* on page 187 to learn how.
3. Touch the application icon. The application description appears.
4. Touch the icon in the upper right-hand corner of the screen. The Application options appear at the bottom of the screen, as shown in **Figure 13**.
5. Touch **Gift**. The Send Gift screen appears, as shown in **Figure 14**.
6. Touch **To:** and enter the email address of the recipient of the gift. Enter an optional message.
7. Touch **Today** to select when the gift should be shared, if the date is other than the current day.
8. Touch **Next** in the upper right-hand corner of the screen. The Theme Selection screen appears.
9. Select a theme and touch **Next** in the upper right-hand corner of the screen. The Gift Confirmation screen appears, as shown in **Figure 15**.
10. Touch **Buy** in the upper right-hand corner of the screen. 'BUY NOW' appears as a confirmation.
11. Touch **BUY NOW**. The password prompt appears.
12. Enter your iTunes password and touch **OK**. The gift is purchased and sent.

Note: You are charged for the gifted application as soon as you purchase it.

Figure 13: Application Options

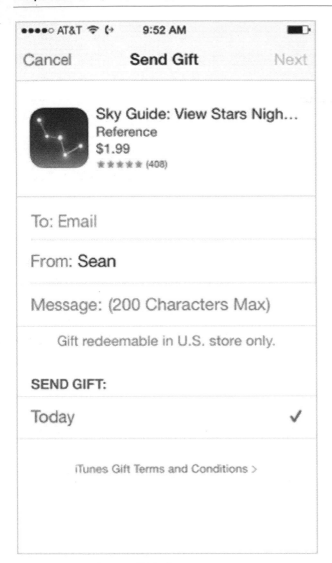

Figure 14: Send Gift Screen

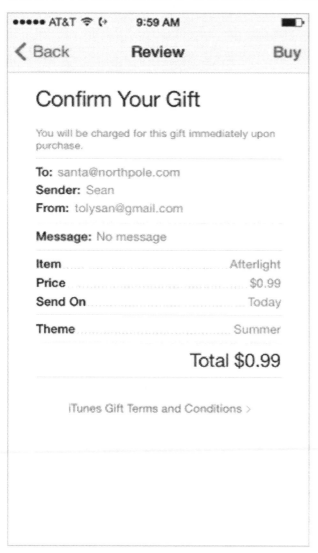

Figure 15: Gift Confirmation Screen

15. Redeeming a Gifted Application

When receiving an application as a gift, you must redeem it in order to download it. To redeem a gift and download the application using your iPhone:

1. Touch the ![icon] icon. The email application opens.
2. Touch the email with the subject **'NAME sent you an iTunes Gift'**, where NAME represents the name of the sender. The email opens. Refer to *"Reading Email"* on page 160 to learn how to find an email.

3. Touch the **Redeem Now** button in the email. The Application Store opens.

4. Touch **Redeem** in the upper right-hand corner of the screen. The gifted application is downloaded and installed. If the application is over 10MB, you must first turn on Wi-Fi. Refer to *"Using Wi-Fi"* on page 24 to learn how to turn Wi-Fi on. If this is your first time downloading an application from the iTunes store, you will need to touch **Agree** several times to accept several pages of terms and conditions.

16. Turning Automatic Application Updates On or Off

The iPhone can automatically download updates for applications when new versions are released. To turn automatic application updates on or off:

1. Touch the ⚙ icon. The Settings screen appears.

2. Scroll down and touch **iTunes & App Store**. The iTunes & App Store Settings screen appears.

3. Touch the ⬤ switch next to 'Updates' under 'Automatic Downloads'. The ◯ switch appears Automatic application updates are turned off.

4. Touch the ◯ switch next to 'Updates' under 'Automatic Downloads'. The ⬤ switch appears Automatic application updates are turned on.

Using Siri

Siri is a voice-activated assistant that comes with the iPhone 5. Follow the tips in this chapter to use Siri to its full potential.

Table of Contents

1. Making a Call

To make a call using Siri, press and hold the **Home** button or hold the phone up to your ear and wait for Siri to speak. Say one of the following phrases:

- **Call John** (use any name)
- **Call Suzy Mobile**
- **Call Dexter on his work phone**
- **Call 123 555 1345**
- **Call home**
- **FaceTime Jacob**

Note: These phrases are only suggestions. Siri is flexible, and you can use many synonymous phrases.

2. Sending and Receiving Text Messages

To send, read, or reply to a text message using Siri, press and hold the **Home** button or hold the phone up to your ear and wait for Siri to speak. Say one of the following phrases:

- **Tell Anne See you soon**
- **Send a message to Rob Burr**
- **Send a message to Larry saying What's your address?**
- **Send a message to Julie on her mobile saying I got an iPhone 5!**
- **Send a message to 999 555 2222**
- **Text Jude and Prudence What are you guys up to today?**
- **Read my new messages**
- **Read it again**
- **Reply that's great news**
- **Tell him ETA is 20 minutes**
- **Call her**

Note: These phrases are only suggestions. Siri is flexible, and you can use many synonymous phrases.

3. Managing the Address Book

To manage the address book using Siri, press and hold the Home button or hold the phone up to your ear and wait for Siri to speak. Say one of the following phrases:

- **What's Joe's address?**
- **What is Susan Park's phone number?**
- **When is my grandfather's birthday?**
- **Show Bobby's email address**
- **Show Pete Abred**
- **Find people named Apple**
- **My brother is Trudy Ages** (assigns a relationship to the name)
- **Who is Colin Card?** (gives Colin Card's contact information)
- **Call my brother at home** (calls the number assigned to the relationship 'brother')

Note: These phrases are only suggestions. Siri is flexible, and you can use many synonymous phrases.

4. Setting Up and Managing Meetings

To set up and manage meetings using Siri, press and hold the **Home** button or hold the phone up to your ear and wait for Siri to speak. Say one of the following phrases:

- **Set up a meeting at 10**
- **Set up a meeting with Zoe at 9**
- **Meet with Nikki at noon**
- **New appointment with Dan Delion Tuesday at 4**
- **Schedule a focus group meeting at 3:30 today in the boardroom**
- **Move my 2pm meeting to 3:30**
- **Add Wendy to my meeting with Waldo**
- **Cancel the focus group meeting**
- **What does the rest of my day look like?**
- **What's on my calendar for Monday?**
- **When is my next appointment?**
- **Where is my next meeting?**

Note: These phrases are only suggestions. Siri is flexible, and you can use many synonymous phrases.

5. Checking the Time and Setting Alarms

To check the time and set alarms using Siri, press and hold the **Home** button or hold the phone up to your ear and wait for Siri to speak. Say one of the following phrases:

- **Wake me up tomorrow at 6am**
- **Set an alarm for 6:30am**
- **Wake me up in 8 hours**
- **Change my 5:30 alarm to 6:30**
- **Turn off my 4:30 alarm**
- **What time is it?**
- **What time is it in Moscow?**
- **What is today's date?**
- **What's the date this Friday?**
- **Set the timer for 30 minutes**
- **Show the timer**
- **Pause the timer**
- **Resume**
- **Reset the timer**
- **Stop the timer**

Note: These phrases are only suggestions. Siri is flexible, and you can use many synonymous phrases.

6. Sending and Receiving Email

To send and receive email using Siri, press and hold the **Home** button or hold the phone up to your ear and wait for Siri to speak. Say one of the following phrases:

- **Email Dave about the trip**
- **Email New email to John Diss**
- **Mail Dad about dinner**
- **Email Dr. Spaulding and say Got your message**
- **Mail Jack and Jill about the party and say It was awesome**
- **Check email**

Note: These phrases are only suggestions. Siri is flexible, and you can use many synonymous phrases.

7. Searching the Web and Asking Questions

To search the Web using Siri, press and hold the **Home** button or hold the phone up to your ear and wait for Siri to speak. Say one of the following phrases:

- **Search the web for Apple News**
- **Search for chili recipes**
- **Google the humane society**
- **Search Wikipedia for Duckbilled Platypus**
- **Bing Secondhand Serenade**
- **How many calories in a doughnut?**
- **What is an 18% tip on $180.45 for six people?**
- **How long do cats live?**
- **What's 25 squared?**
- **How many dollars is 60 euros?**
- **How many days until Christmas?**
- **When is the next solar eclipse?**
- **Show me the Ursula Major constellation**
- **What is the meaning of life?**
- **What's the price of gasoline in Boston?**

Note: These phrases are only suggestions. Siri is flexible, and you can use many synonymous phrases.

8. Looking Up Words in the Dictionary

To look up words using Siri, press and hold the **Home** button or hold the phone up to your ear and wait for Siri to speak. Say one of the following phrases:

- **What is the meaning of meticulous?**
- **Define albeit**
- **Look up the word jargon**

Note: These phrases are only suggestions. Siri is flexible, and you can use many phrases synonymous with these suggestions.

Adjusting the Settings

Table of Contents

Adjusting Wireless Settings

Table of Contents

1. Turning Airplane Mode On or Off

Most airplanes do not allow wireless communications while in flight. Continue using the iPhone by enabling Airplane mode before take-off. You may not place or receive calls, send or receive text messages or emails, or surf the Web while in Airplane mode. Airplane Mode is also useful when traveling outside of your area of service to avoid any roaming charges and to preserve battery life. To turn Airplane Mode on or off:

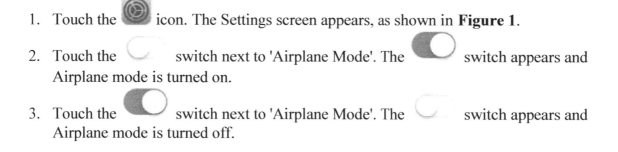

1. Touch the ⦿ icon. The Settings screen appears, as shown in **Figure 1**.

2. Touch the ⬭ switch next to 'Airplane Mode'. The 🔘 switch appears and Airplane mode is turned on.

3. Touch the 🔘 switch next to 'Airplane Mode'. The ⬭ switch appears and Airplane mode is turned off.

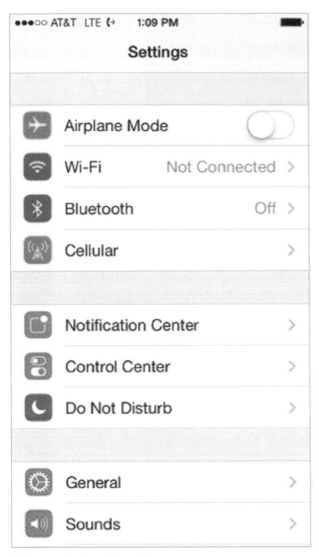

Figure 1: Settings Screen

2. Turning Location Services On or Off

Some iPhone applications require the Location Services feature to be turned on, which determines your current location. To turn Location Services on or off:

1. Touch the ⚙ icon. The Settings screen appears.
2. Scroll down and touch **Privacy**. The Privacy Settings screen appears, as shown in **Figure 2**.
3. Touch **Location Services**. The Location Services screen appears, as shown in **Figure 3**.

4. Touch the ⬤ switch next to 'Location Services'. The ⬤ switch appears and Location Services are turned on.

5. Touch the ⬤ switch next to 'Location Services'. The ⬤ switch appears and Location Services are turned off.

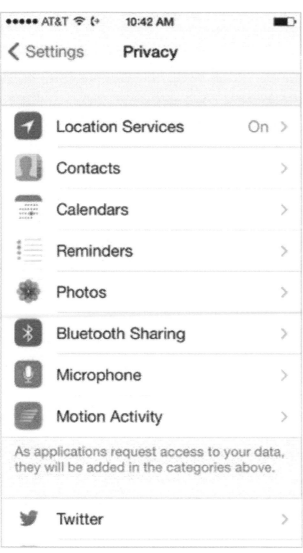

Figure 2: Privacy Settings Screen

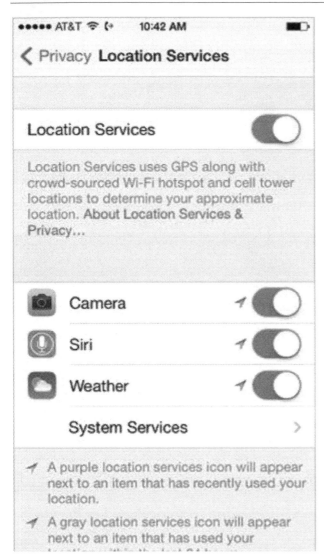

Figure 3: Location Services Screen

3. Turning 4G On or Off

Using the 4G network will allow data to be accessed faster than on 2G. Surfing the internet and downloading applications is also faster. However, you can turn 4G off if you wish to conserve battery life. To turn 4G on or off:

1. Touch the ⬤ icon. The Settings screen appears.

2. Touch **Cellular**. The Cellular Settings screen appears, as shown in **Figure 4**.

3. Touch the ⬭ switch next to 'Enable 4G'. The ⬤ switch appears and 3G is turned on.

4. Touch the ⬤ switch next to 'Enable 4G'. The ⬭ switch appears and 3G is turned off.

Note: Turning 4G on in an area where AT&T or Verizon has no 4G coverage will result in the iPhone's having no access to the wireless network. This will result in the iPhone's battery dying more quickly, as it will continue to search for service. In this case, simply turn 4G off to regain normal 2G coverage.

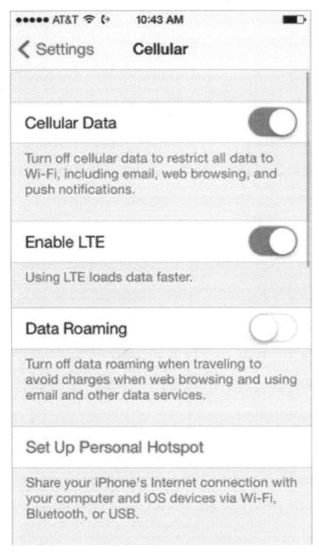

Figure 4: Cellular Settings Screen

4. Turning Data Roaming On or Off

When you are in an area with no wireless coverage, the iPhone can use the Data Roaming feature to acquire signal from other networks. Be aware that Data Roaming can be extremely costly. Contact your network provider for details. To turn Data Roaming on or off:

1. Touch the ⬤ icon. The Settings screen appears.
2. Touch **Cellular**. The Cellular Settings screen appears.
3. Touch the ⬤ switch next to 'Data Roaming'. The ⬤ switch appears and Data Roaming is turned on.

4. Touch the ⬤ switch next to 'Data Roaming'. The ⬭ switch appears and Data Roaming is turned off.

5. Setting Up a Virtual Private Network (VPN)

You can use your iPhone to connect to an external network, such as a corporate one. To set up a VPN:

1. Touch the ⬤ icon. The Settings screen appears.
2. Touch **General**. The General Settings screen appears.
3. Touch **VPN**. The VPN screen appears, as shown in **Figure 5**.
4. Touch the ⬭ switch next to 'VPN'. The Add Configuration screen appears, as shown in **Figure 6**.
5. Touch each field and enter the required information. Touch **Save** in the upper right-hand corner of the screen when you are finished. The VPN is set up.

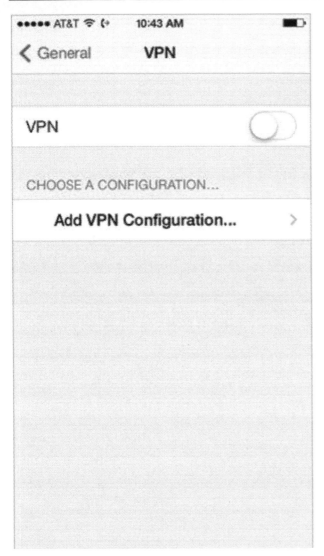

Figure 5: VPN Screen

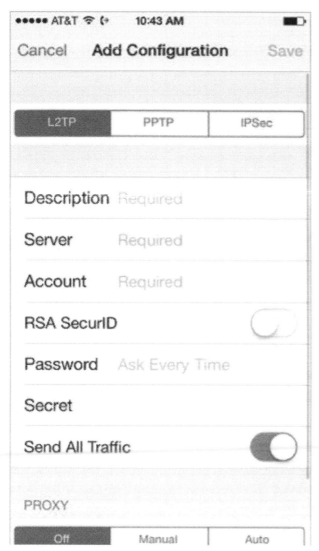

Figure 6: Add Configuration Screen

---

6. Turning Bluetooth On or Off

A wireless Bluetooth headset can be used with the iPhone. Be aware that leaving Bluetooth turned on while the headset is not in use eats up a lot of battery life. To turn Bluetooth on or off:

1. Touch the ⚙ icon. The Settings screen appears.
2. Touch **General**. The General Settings screen appears.
3. Touch **Bluetooth**. The Bluetooth Settings screen appears, as shown in **Figure** 7.
4. Touch the ⬭ switch next to 'Bluetooth'. Bluetooth is turned on and a list of devices appears. If there are no Bluetooth devices near the iPhone, the list will be empty.

5. Touch the 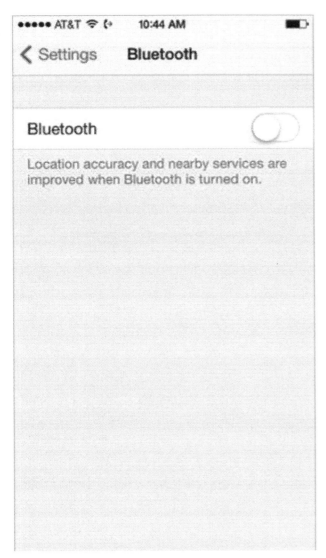 switch next to 'Bluetooth'. Bluetooth is turned off.

Figure 7: Bluetooth Settings Screen

Adjusting Sound Settings

Table of Contents

1. Turning Vibration On or Off

The iPhone can be set to vibrate every time it rings or only while it is in Silent Mode.
To turn Ringer Vibration on or off:

1. Touch the ⚙ icon. The Settings screen appears, as shown in **Figure 1**.
2. Scroll down and touch **Sounds**. The Sound Settings screen appears, as shown in **Figure 2**.
3. Touch the ⬜ switch next to 'Vibrate on Ring' under the 'Vibrate' section. The 🔵 switch appears and Ringer Vibration is turned on. The iPhone will vibrate whenever there is an incoming call.
4. Touch the 🔵 switch. Ringer Vibration is turned off and the iPhone will not vibrate for incoming calls.

To turn Silent Mode vibration on or off:

1. Touch the ⚙ icon. The Settings screen appears.
2. Touch **Sounds**. The Sound Settings screen appears.
3. Touch the ⬜ switch next to 'Vibrate on Silent' under the 'Vibrate' section.

The 🔵 switch appears and Silent Mode vibration is turned on. The iPhone will vibrate whenever a call or message is received in Silent Mode.

4. Touch the switch. Silent Mode Vibration is turned off. The iPhone will not vibrate when it is in Silent Mode.

Note: To turn on Silent Mode on the iPhone, put the vibration switch in the down position so that a red dot appears. Silent mode is turned on and the icon appears on the screen. Refer to "Button Layout" on page 9 to view the location of the Vibration switch.

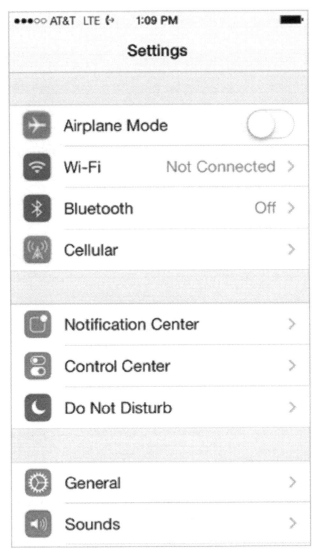

Figure 1: Settings Screen

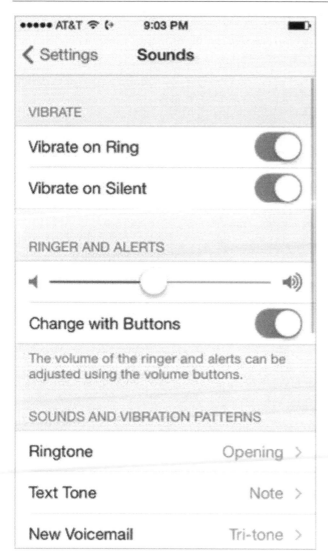

Figure 2: Sound Settings Screen

---

2. Turning Volume Button Functionality On or Off

The volume buttons can be used to adjust the volume of the media, alerts, and the ringer. When the volume button functionality is disabled, they no longer work. To turn the volume button functionality on or off:

1. Touch the ![icon] icon. The Settings screen appears.
2. Scroll down and touch **Sounds**. The Sound Settings screen appears.

3. Touch the ⬤ switch next to 'Change with Buttons' under the 'Ringer and Alerts' section. The ◯ switch appears and volume button functionality is turned off.

4. Touch the ◯ switch next to 'Change with Buttons'. The ⬤ switch appears and the volume button functionality is turned on.

3. Setting the Default Ringtone

You may change the ringtone that sounds every time somebody calls you. To set a default ringtone:

1. Touch the ⊚ icon. The Settings screen appears.
2. Touch **Sounds**. The Sound Settings screen appears.
3. Touch **Ringtone** under the 'Sounds and Vibration Patterns' section. A list of ringtones appears, as shown in **Figure 3**.
4. Touch a ringtone. The new default ringtone is selected and a preview plays.
5. Touch **Sounds** in the upper left-hand corner of the screen. The new ringtone is set as the default.

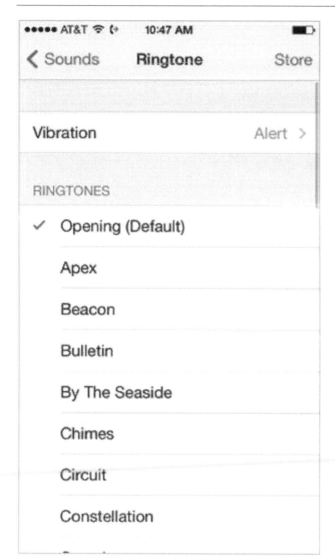

Figure 3: List of Ringtones

4. Customizing Notification and Alert Sounds

There are several notification and alert sounds that can be changed on the iPhone. To customize notification and alert sounds:

1. Touch the ⚙ icon. The Settings screen appears.
2. Touch **Sounds**. The Sound Settings screen appears.
3. Touch one of the following options under the 'Sounds and Vibration Patterns' section to change the corresponding sound:

- **Text Tone** - Plays when a new text message arrives.
- **New Voicemail** - Plays when a new voicemail arrives.
- **New Mail** - Plays when a new email arrives.
- **Sent Mail** - Plays when an email is sent from the iPhone.
- **Tweet** - Plays when a new Tweet arrives.
- **Facebook Post** - Plays when one of your Facebook friends creates a new post.
- **Calendar Alerts** - Plays as a reminder for a calendar event.
- **Reminder Alerts** - Plays as a notification of a previously set reminder.

5. Turning Lock Sounds On or Off

The iPhone can make a sound every time it is locked or unlocked. By default, this sound is turned on. To turn Lock Sounds on or off:

1. Touch the ⚙ icon. The Settings screen appears.
2. Touch **Sounds**. The Sound Settings screen appears.
3. Scroll down and touch the ⬤ switch next to 'Lock Sounds'. The ⬤ switch appears and lock sounds are turned off.
4. Touch the ⬤ switch next to 'Lock Sounds'. The ⬤ switch appears and lock sounds are turned on.

6. Turning Keyboard Clicks On or Off

The iPhone can make a sound every time a key is touched on the virtual keyboard. By default, keyboard clicks are turned on. To turn Keyboard Clicks on or off:

1. Touch the ⚙ icon. The Settings screen appears.
2. Touch **Sounds**. The Sound Settings screen appears.
3. Touch the ⬤ switch next to 'Keyboard Clicks'. The ⬤ switch appears and Keyboard Clicks are turned off.
4. Touch the ⬤ switch next to 'Keyboard Clicks'. The ⬤ switch appears and Keyboard Clicks are turned on.

Adjusting Language and Keyboard Settings

Table of Contents

1. Customizing Spelling and Grammar Settings

Customize the Spelling and Grammar settings on your iPhone to improve typing accuracy when composing text messages or emails. To customize the Spelling and Grammar settings:

1. Touch the ⚙ icon. The Settings screen appears, as shown in **Figure 1**.
2. Touch **General**. The General Settings screen appears, as shown in **Figure 2**.
3. Scroll down and touch **Keyboard**. The Keyboard Settings screen appears, as shown in **Figure 3**.
4. Touch one of the following switches on the right side of the screen to turn the corresponding setting on or off:

   - **Auto-Capitalization** - Capitalizes the first word of every sentence automatically.
   - **Auto-Correction** - Suggests and makes text corrections while you type.
   - **Check Spelling** - Underlines all misspelled words.

   - **Enable Caps Lock** - Allows you to turn Caps Lock on by quickly touching the ⇧ key twice on the virtual keyboard. While Caps Lock is turned on, all capital letters are typed without the need to use the ⇧ key.
   - **."" Shortcut** - Allows a period and an extra space to be inserted when you quickly touch the space bar twice.

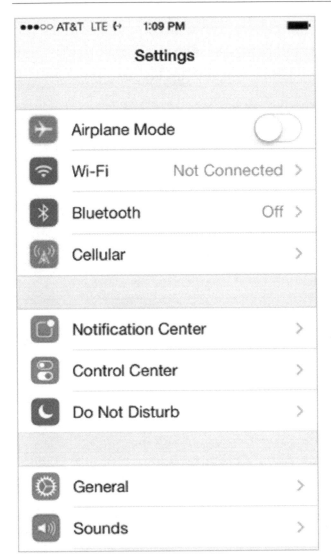

Figure 1: Settings Screen

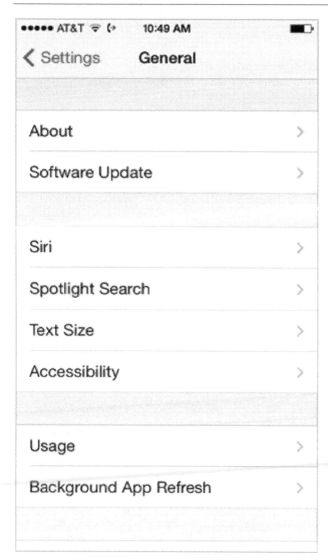

Figure 2: General Settings Screen

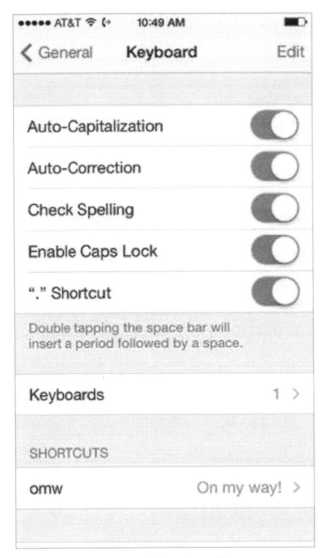

Figure 3: Keyboard Settings Screen

2. Adding an International Keyboard

The iPhone allows you to use international keyboards when entering text on the virtual keyboard. To add an international keyboard:

1. Touch the ⚙ icon. The Settings screen appears.
2. Touch **General**. The General Settings screen appears.
3. Scroll down and touch **Keyboard**. The Keyboard Settings screen appears.
4. Touch **Keyboards**. The Keyboards screen appears, as shown in **Figure 4**.

5. Touch **Add New Keyboard**. A list of international keyboards appears, as shown in **Figure 5**.

6. Touch a keyboard. The keyboard is added. While typing, touch the 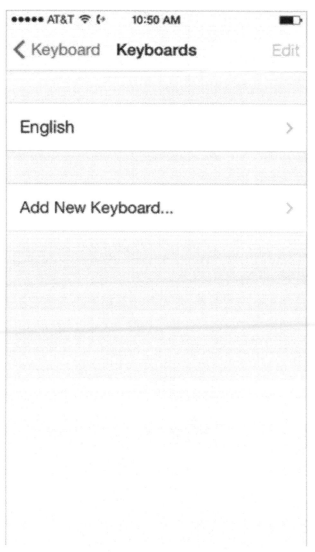 key at the bottom of the virtual keyboard to switch to an international one.

Figure 4: Keyboards Screen

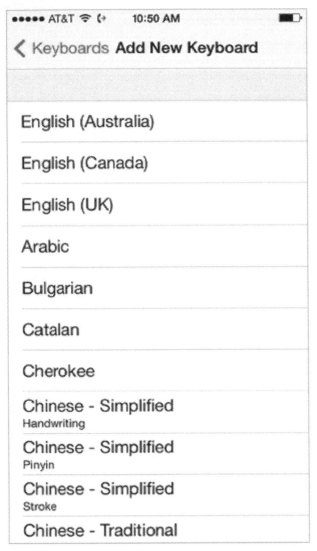

Figure 5: List of International Keyboards

3. Adding a Keyboard Shortcut

The iPhone allows you to add custom Keyboard shortcuts. For example, "ur" for "your" or "ttyl" for "talk to you later" are substituted when the corresponding abbreviation is typed. To add a Keyboard shortcut:

1. Touch the 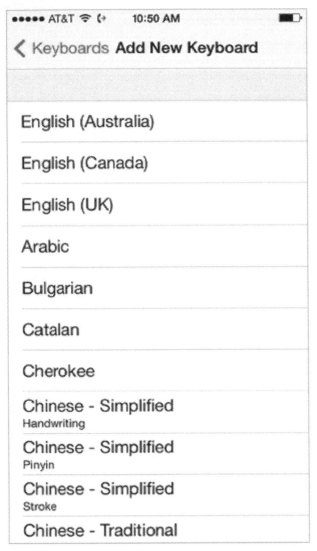 icon. The Settings screen appears.
2. Touch **General**. The General Settings screen appears.
3. Scroll down and touch **Keyboard**. The Keyboard Settings screen appears.

4. Touch **Add New Shortcut** under the 'Shortcuts' section. The Shortcut screen appears, as shown in **Figure 6**.
5. Enter the desired phrase to be substituted for the shortcut. Touch **return**.
6. Enter the desired shortcut and touch **Save** in the upper right-hand corner of the screen. The keyboard shortcut is added. To use the shortcut, type it and touch the space bar.

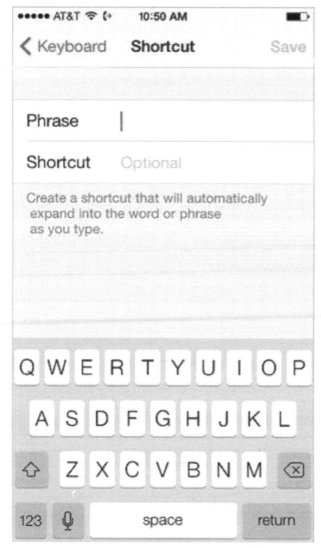

Figure 6: Shortcut Screen

4. Changing the Operating System Language

The iOS on the iPhone can be changed to display all menus and options in a language other than English. To change the Operating System Language:

1. Touch the ⊚ icon. The Settings screen appears.
2. Touch **General**. The General Settings screen appears.
3. Scroll down and touch **International**. The International screen appears, as shown in **Figure 7**.
4. Touch **Language**. A list of available languages appears, as shown in **Figure 8**.
5. Touch a language and touch **Done** in the upper right-hand corner of the screen. The selected language is applied and all menus and options reflect the change.

Note: It may take some time to install the language. This delay is normal.'

Figure 7: International Screen

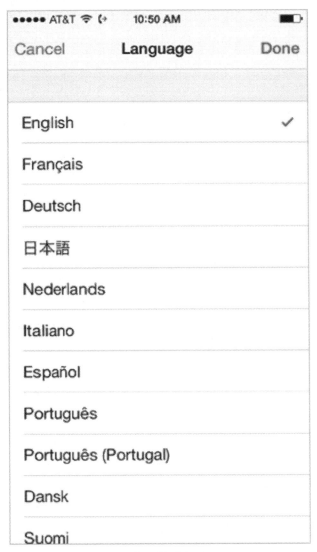

Figure 8: List of Available Languages

5. Changing the Siri Language

You can change the input language that Siri recognizes as well as the language that she uses to speak. To change the Siri language:

1. Touch the ⬡ icon. The Settings screen appears.
2. Touch **General**. The General Settings screen appears.
3. Scroll down and touch **International**. The International screen appears.
4. Touch **Voice Control**. A list of languages appears.
5. Touch a language. The selected language will be used for Voice Control input.
6. Touch **International** in the upper left-hand corner of the screen. Your language selection is saved.

Note: Press and hold the **Home** *button to activate Siri. The Siri screen appears, as shown in* **Figure 9**.

Figure 9: Voice Control Screen

6. Changing the Keyboard Layout

The layout of the keyboard in most languages can be changed, according to personal preference. For instance, the English keyboard can be set display in default QWERTY, as shown in **Figure 10**, AZERTY, as shown in **Figure 11**, or QWERTZ as shown in **Figure 12**. To change the Keyboard Layout:

1. Touch the ⚙ icon. The Settings screen appears.
2. Touch **General**. The General Settings screen appears.
3. Scroll down and touch **Keyboard**. The Keyboard Settings screen appears.

4. Touch the language of the keyboard you wish to change. The Keyboard Layout screen appears.
5. Touch the desired layout. The new Keyboard Layout is set.

Figure 10: QWERTY Keyboard

Figure 11: AZERTY Keyboard

Figure 12: QWERTZ Keyboard

7. Changing the Region Format

The region format on the iPhone determines how dates, times, and phone numbers are universally displayed. For instance, a European country may display the 30th day of the first month in the year 2011 as 30/01/2011, whereas the U.S. would display the same date as 01/30/2011. To change the region format:

1. Touch the ⚙ icon. The Settings screen appears.
2. Touch **General**. The General Settings screen appears.
3. Touch **International**. The International screen appears.
4. Touch **Region Format**. A list of region formats appears, as shown in **Figure 13**.
5. Touch the desired format. The new format is set.
6. Touch **International** in the upper left-hand corner of the screen. The new region format is saved.

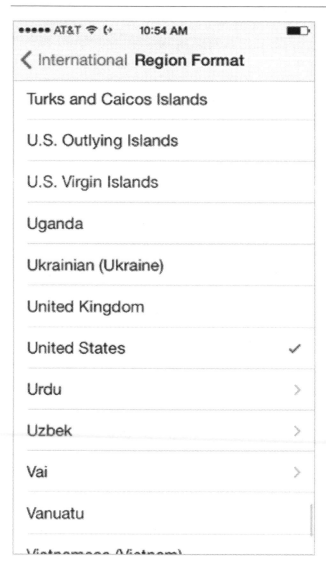

Figure 13: List of Region Formats

Adjusting General Settings

Table of Contents

1. Changing Auto-Lock Settings

The iPhone can lock itself when it is idle in order to save battery life and to avoid unintentionally pressing buttons. When it is locked, the iPhone can still receive calls and text messages. By default, the iPhone is set to automatically lock after one minute. To change the length of time that will pass before the iPhone locks itself:

1. Touch the icon. The Settings screen appears, as shown in **Figure 1**.
2. Touch **General**. The General Settings screen appears, as shown in **Figure 2**.
3. Scroll down and touch **Auto-Lock**. The Auto-Lock Settings screen appears, as shown in **Figure 3**.
4. Touch an amount of time or touch **Never** if you do not want the iPhone to automatically lock itself. The change is applied and the iPhone will wait the selected amount of time before automatically locking itself.

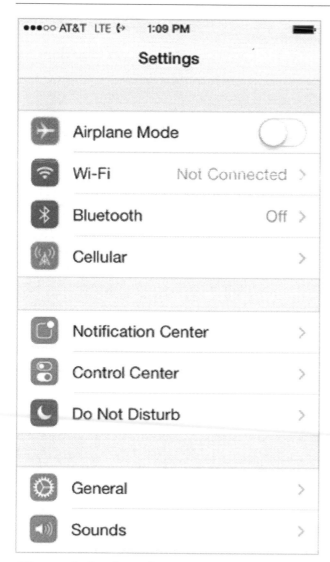

Figure 1: Settings Screen

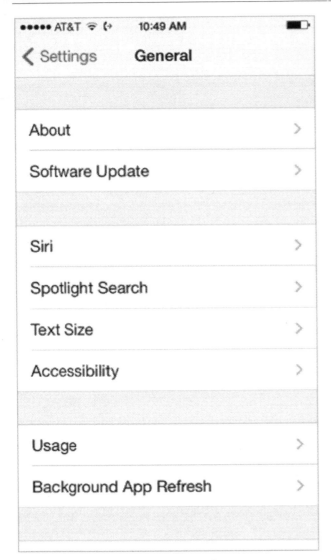

Figure 2: General Settings Screen

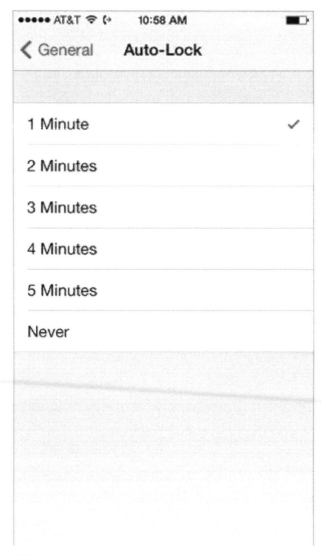

Figure 3: Auto-Lock Settings Screen

2. Adjusting the Brightness

You may wish to increase the brightness of the screen on your iPhone when you are in a sunny area. On the other hand, you may wish to decrease the brightness in a dark area to conserve battery life. You can also turn Auto-Brightness on or off, which will determine whether or not the iPhone automatically sets the brightness based on the lighting conditions. To adjust the brightness:

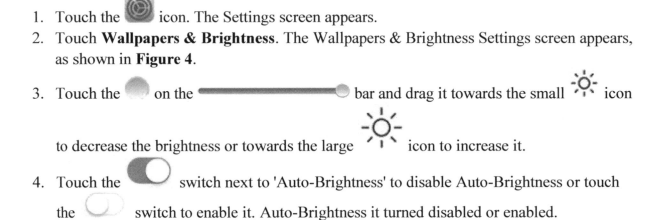

1. Touch the   icon. The Settings screen appears.
2. Touch **Wallpapers & Brightness**. The Wallpapers & Brightness Settings screen appears, as shown in **Figure 4**.
3. Touch the   on the   bar and drag it towards the small   icon to decrease the brightness or towards the large   icon to increase it.
4. Touch the   switch next to 'Auto-Brightness' to disable Auto-Brightness or touch the   switch to enable it. Auto-Brightness it turned disabled or enabled.

Note: While Auto-Brightness is enabled, you can still temporarily adjust the brightness of the screen. However, as soon as the lighting conditions change, the iPhone will automatically change the brightness.

Figure 4: Wallpapers & Brightness Settings Screen

3. Assigning a Passcode Lock or Fingerprint Lock

The iPhone can prompt for a four-digit or alphanumeric password, or your fingerprint before unlocking.

To set up a password lock:

1. Touch the icon. The Settings screen appears.
2. Touch **General**. The General Settings screen appears.

3. Touch **Passcode & Fingerprint**. The Passcode & Fingerprint screen appears, as shown in **Figure 5**.

4. Touch **Turn Passcode On**. The Set Passcode screen appears, as shown in **Figure 6**, if the Simple Passcode feature is turned on. The Set Password screen appears, as shown in **Figure 7**, if the Simple Passcode feature is turned off.

5. Enter a passcode. A confirmation screen appears.

6. Enter the passcode again. The new passcode is set.

7. Touch one of the following options on the Passcode Lock screen to change the corresponding setting:

- **Require Passcode** - Set the time the iPhone waits before asking the user for the passcode. It is recommended to choose the default, **Immediately**, since an unauthorized user will not have access to your iPhone for any period of time if this option is chosen. Choosing one of the other options causes the iPhone to wait a set amount of time after being locked before requiring a passcode.

- **Simple Passcode** - Allows you to enter a four-digit passcode. When turned off, you must enter an alphanumeric password when setting the passcode.

- **Erase Data** - Erases all data after a user enters the passcode incorrectly ten times in a row.

Warning: You will not be able to recover your data if this feature is on when an incorrect passcode is entered ten times consecutively.

To set up a fingerprint lock:

1. Set up a password lock. Refer to the instructions above to learn how.

2. Touch **Fingerprints**. The Fingerprints screen appears, as shown in **Figure 8**.

3. Touch **Add a fingerprint**. The Fingerprint Setup screen appears.

4. Touch (do not press) the Home button with the finger that you use to press the Home button.

5. Lift and rest your finger on the Home button repeatedly. Keep doing this until the Fingerprint Confirmation screen appears, as shown in **Figure 9**. Your fingerprint can now be used to unlock the iPhone. To unlock the iPhone, activate the screen and scan your fingerprint.

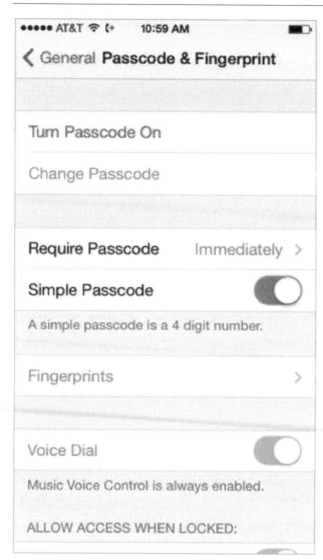

Figure 5: Passcode & Fingerprint Screen

Figure 6: Set Passcode Screen

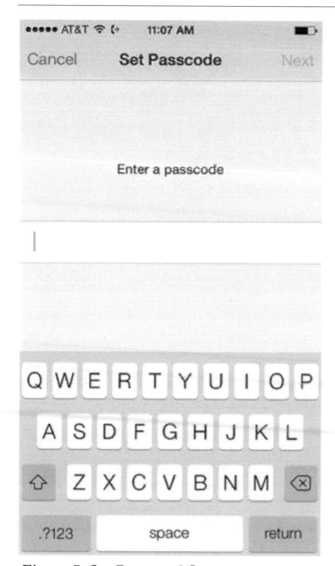

Figure 7: Set Password Screen

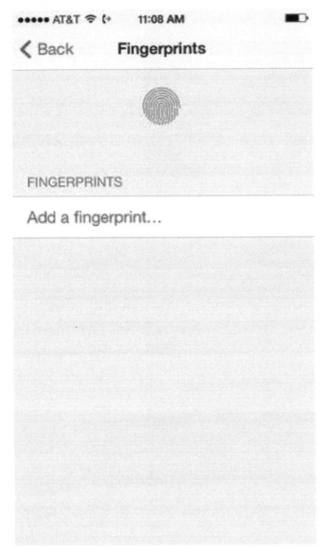

Figure 8: Fingerprints Screen

Figure 9: Fingerprint Confirmation Screen

3. Turning 24-Hour Mode On or Off

The iPhone can display the time in regular 12-hour mode or in 24-hour mode, commonly referred to as military time. To turn 24-hour mode on or off:

1. Touch the ⚙ icon. The Settings screen appears.
2. Touch **General**. The General Settings screen appears.

3. Scroll down and touch **Date & Time**. The Date & Time screen appears, as shown in **Figure 10**.

4. Touch the ⬭ switch next to '24-Hour Time'. The ⬬ switch appears 24-Hour mode is turned on.

5. Touch the ⬬ switch next to '24-Hour Time'. The ⬭ switch appears and 24-Hour mode is turned off.

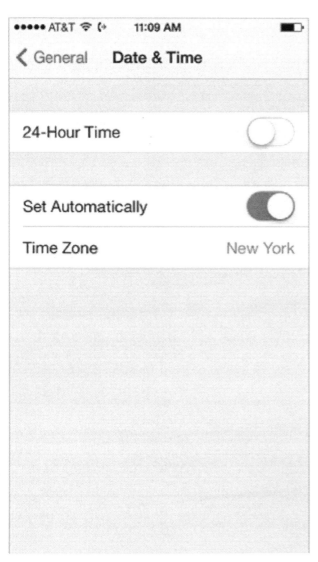

Figure 10: Date & Time Screen

4. Resetting the Home Screen Layout

You can reset the Home screen on your iPhone to look like it did when you first purchased it. To reset the Home Screen Layout:

Note: Resetting the Home screen layout does not delete any applications, but simply rearranges them.

1. Touch the icon. The Settings screen appears.
2. Touch **General**. The General Settings screen appears.
3. Scroll down and touch **Reset**. The Reset screen appears, as shown in **Figure 11**.
4. Touch **Reset Home Screen Layout**. A confirmation appears at the bottom of the screen.
5. Touch **Reset Home Screen**. The Home Screen Layout is reset.

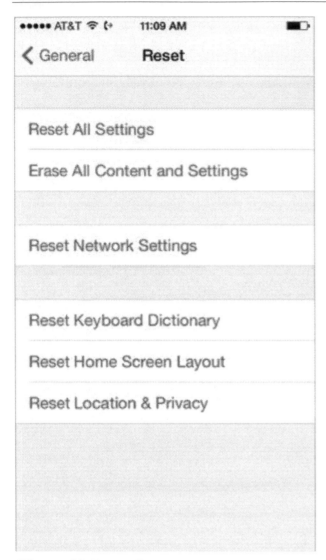

Figure 11: Reset Screen

5. Resetting All Settings

You can reset all of the settings on your iPhone to the state they were in when you first purchased it. To reset all settings:

Note: Resetting the settings will NOT delete any data from your iPhone.

1. Touch the ⚙ icon. The Settings screen appears.
2. Touch **General**. The General Settings screen appears.
3. Scroll down and touch **Reset**. The Reset screen appears.
4. Touch **Reset All Settings**. A confirmation appears at the bottom of the screen. You will also need to enter your passcode, if you have one.
5. Touch **Reset All Settings**. All settings are reset to defaults.

6. Erasing and Restoring the iPhone

You can delete all of the data and reset all settings to completely restore the iPhone to its original condition. To erase and restore the iPhone to its original condition:

Warning: Any erased data is not recoverable. Make sure you back up all of the data you wish to keep.

1. Touch the ⚙ icon. The Settings screen appears.
2. Touch **General**. The General Settings screen appears.
3. Touch **Reset**. The Reset screen appears.
4. Touch **Erase All Content and Settings**. A confirmation appears at the bottom of the screen.
5. Touch **Erase iPhone**. Data on the iPhone is erased, and the iPhone is restored to its original condition.

Adjusting Accessibility Settings

Table of Contents

1. Managing Vision Accessibility Features

Vision accessibility features allow people with visual disabilities to use the iPhone with greater ease. To manage vision accessibility features:

1. Touch the ⚙ icon. The Settings screen appears, as shown in **Figure 1**.
2. Touch **General**. The General Settings screen appears, as shown in **Figure 2**.
3. Touch **Accessibility**. The Accessibility Settings screen appears, as shown in **Figure 3**.
4. Touch one of the following options to turn vision accessibility features on or off:

   - **VoiceOver** - This feature speaks an item on the screen when you touch it once, activates it when you touch it twice, and scrolls through a list or page of text when you touch the screen with three fingers.
   - **Zoom** - This features zooms in on an item when you touch the screen twice using three fingers, moves around when you drag three fingers on the screen, and changes the level of zoom when you touch the screen with three fingers twice and drag.
   - **Invert Colors** - This feature inverts all of the colors on the screen. For instance, black text on a white screen becomes white text on a black screen.
   - **Speak Selection** - This feature allows all text on the screen to be spoken aloud when you select it and touch **Speak**.
   - **Speak Auto-text** - This feature speaks every auto-correction or auto-capitalization as you enter text in any text field, including text messages and emails.
   - **Larger Type** - This feature increases the default size of the font. Use the font slider to adjust the default font size.
   - **Bold Text** - This feature makes all text on the iPhone bold in order to make it easier to read. Enabling or disabling this feature requires you to restart the iPhone.

- **Increase Contrast** - This feature improves the contrast on certain backgrounds in order to make it easier to read certain text.

- **On/Off Labels** - This feature turns [switch] and [switch] switches into [switch] and [switch] switches, respectively.

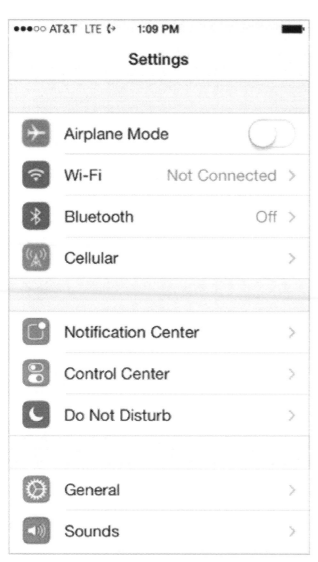

Figure 1: Settings Screen

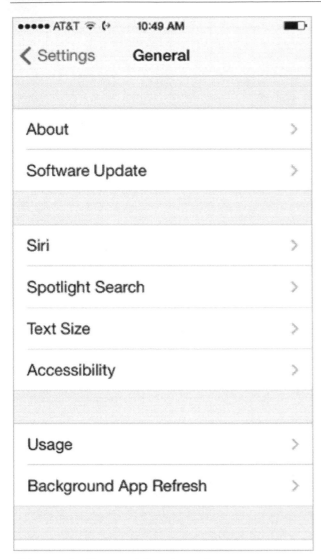

Figure 2: General Settings Screen

Figure 3: Accessibility Settings Screen

2. Managing Hearing Accessibility Features

Hearing accessibility features allow people with hearing disabilities to use the iPhone with greater ease. To manage hearing accessibility features:

1. Touch the ⚙ icon. The Settings screen appears.
2. Touch **General**. The General Settings screen appears.
3. Touch **Accessibility**. The Accessibility Settings screen appears.
4. Touch one of the following options to turn hearing accessibility features on or off:

- **Hearing Aid Mode** - This feature automatically manages the antenna in the iPhone to avoid interference with standard hearing aids and improve overall performance. However, cellular reception may be reduced when using this feature.
- **Subtitles & Captioning** - This feature allows subtitles and closed captioning to be enabled for videos, where available.
- **LED Flash for Alerts** - This feature allows the camera flash to be used to provide notification alerts, such as incoming calls or text messages.
- **Mono Audio** - This feature turns off stereo audio, leaving only one speaker working.

3. Turning Guided Access On or Off

Guided Access is a feature that is made for people with learning disabilities, allowing the user to stay in a single application and control the features that are available. To turn Guided Access on or off:

1. Touch the ⦿ icon. The Settings screen appears.
2. Touch **General**. The General Settings screen appears.
3. Touch **Accessibility**. The Accessibility Settings screen appears.
4. Scroll down and touch **Guided Access**. The Guided Access Settings screen appears, as shown in **Figure 4**.
5. Touch the ⬯ switch next to 'Guided Access'. Guided Access is turned on.
6. Touch **Set Passcode** to set up a passcode that will allow you to exit the application when you done using it.

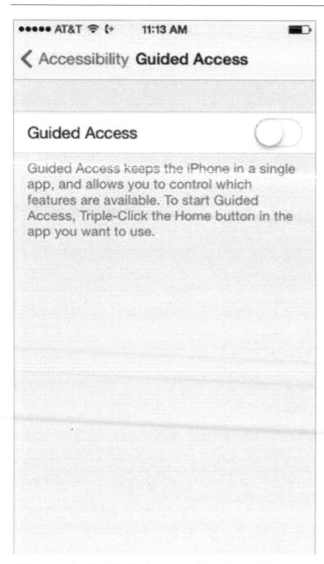

Figure 4: Guided Access Settings Screen

4. Managing Physical & Motor Accessibility Features

Physical and Motor accessibility features allow people with motor disabilities to use the iPhone with greater ease. To manage physical & motor accessibility features:

1. Touch the icon. The Settings screen appears.
2. Touch **General**. The General Settings screen appears.
3. Touch **Accessibility**. The Accessibility Settings screen appears.
4. Touch one of the following options to turn physical and motor accessibility features on or off:

   - **Switch Control** - This feature allows an adaptive accessory to be used to highlight items on the screen to control the functions of the iPhone. The Switch Control screen allows various settings, such as timing, switch stabilization, point scanning, audio, and visual settings, to be adjusted.
   - **Assistive Touch** - This feature allows you to create custom gestures in order to access various services on the iPhone.
   - **Home-click Speed** - This feature allows you to slow down the speed at which you need to press the Home button to access certain features.
   - **Incoming Calls** - This feature allows you to answer calls directly on your headset or speakerphone by default.

Adjusting Phone Settings

Table of Contents

1. Turning Call Forwarding On or Off

The iPhone can be set to forward all calls to a specified number. To turn Call Forwarding on or off:

1. Touch the ⚙ icon. The Settings screen appears, as shown in **Figure 1**.
2. Scroll down and touch **Phone**. The Phone Settings screen appears, as shown in **Figure 2**.
3. Touch **Call Forwarding**. The Call Forwarding screen appears.
4. Touch the ⬭ switch next to 'Call Forwarding'. The 'Forward to' field appears, as shown in **Figure 3**.
5. Touch **Forward to**. The Forwarding To screen appears.
6. Use the keypad to enter the phone number to which the phone should forward. When finished, touch **Back** in the upper left-hand corner of the screen. Call Forwarding is setup and the Call Forwarding screen appears.

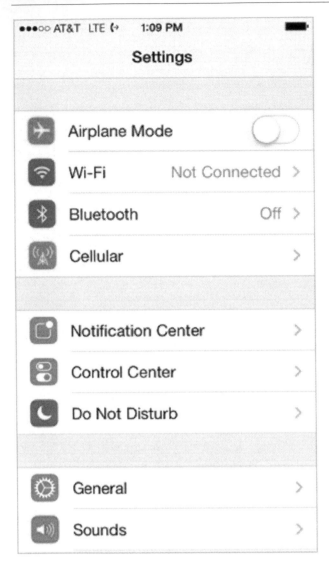

Figure 1: Settings Screen

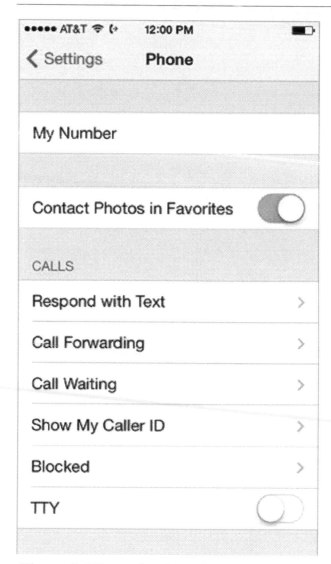

Figure 2: Phone Settings Screen

Figure 3: Forwarding To Screen

---

2. Turning Call Waiting On or Off

While you are on the line with someone, the Call Waiting feature allows the iPhone to alert you when there is a second incoming call. To turn Call Waiting on or off:

1. Touch the icon. The Settings screen appears.
2. Scroll down and touch **Phone**. The Phone Settings screen appears.
3. Touch **Call Waiting**. The Call Waiting screen appears, as shown in **Figure 4**.

4. Touch the ⬤▬ switch next to 'Call Waiting'. The ▬◯ switch appears and Call Waiting is turned off.

5. Touch the ◯▬ switch next to 'Call Waiting'. The ▬⬤ switch appears and Call Waiting is turned on.

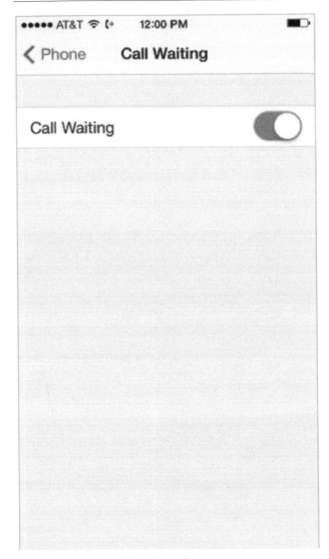

Figure 4: Call Waiting Screen

3. Turning Caller ID On or Off

The Caller ID feature shows your phone number or name (if your number is stored in the recipient's Phonebook) on the called party's device. In order to preserve privacy and make your phone number appear as "Private Number", turn the Caller ID feature off. To turn Caller ID on or off:

1. Touch the ⚙ icon. The Settings screen appears.
2. Scroll down and touch **Phone**. The Phone Settings screen appears.

3. Touch **Show My Caller ID**. The Show My Caller ID screen appears, as shown in **Figure 5**.

4. Touch the ⬤ switch next to 'Show My Caller ID'. The ⬭ switch appears and Caller ID is turned off.

5. Touch the ⬭ switch next to 'Show My Caller ID'. The ⬤ switch appears and Caller ID is turned on.

Note: When Caller ID is turned off, even those who have your phone number stored in their Phonebook will not be able to view your number when receiving a call from you.

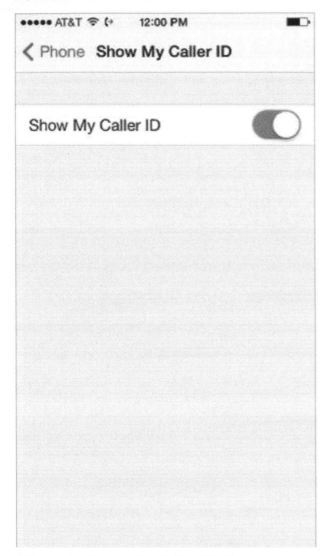

Figure 5: Show My Caller ID Screen

4. Turning TTY Mode On or Off

TTY stands for 'text telephone' or 'teletypewriter'. Using a special TTY machine when this mode is enabled allows speech and hearing impaired users to read incoming speech as text and type responses. The typed text is converted to speech on the other side of the conversation.

Search **Google for TTY machine** to purchase one. You will also need an Apple TTY Adapter, which can be purchased in the online Apple Store, in order to plug in a TTY machine to the iPhone. To turn TTY Mode on or off:

1. Touch the ⬤ icon. The Settings screen appears.
2. Scroll down and touch **Phone**. The Phone Settings screen appears.

3. Touch the ⬭ switch next to 'TTY'. The ⬤ switch appears and TTY mode is turned on.

4. Touch the ⬤ switch next to 'TTY'. The ⬭ switch appears and TTY mode is turned off.

5. Turning the International Assist On or Off

The International Assist feature is useful while traveling abroad. This feature will automatically add the correct international prefix to every phone number you dial when calling a U.S. phone number. To turn International Assist on or off:

1. Touch the ⬤ icon. The Settings screen appears.
2. Scroll down and touch **Phone**. The Phone Settings screen appears.

3. Touch the ⬭ switch next to 'Dial Assist'. The ⬤ switch appears and International Assist is turned on.

4. Touch the ⬤ switch next to 'Dial Assist'. The ⬭ switch appears and International Assist is turned off.

Note: The International Assist feature does not work in all areas.

6. Blocking Specified Numbers

The iPhone can block contacts with specified numbers from calling or texting you. In order to block a number, you must first add it to your Phonebook. To specify numbers to block:

1. Touch the ⬤ icon. The Settings screen appears.
2. Scroll down and touch **Phone**. The Phone Settings screen appears.
3. Touch **Blocked**. The Blocked Numbers screen appears, as shown in **Figure 6**.
4. Touch **Add New**. Your Phonebook appears.
5. Touch a contact. The contact's number is added to the Blocked list.

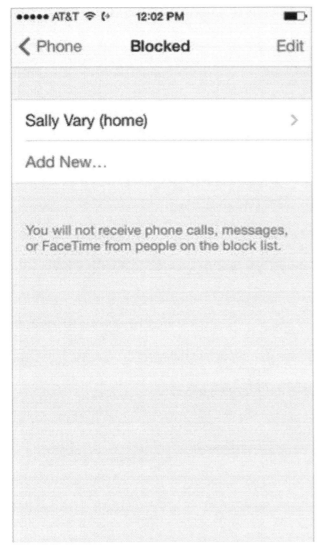

Figure 6: Blocked Numbers Screen

7. Editing Preset Text Message Responses

The iPhone allows you to respond with a preset text if you are unable to answer a call. To edit the preset text message responses:

1. Touch the icon. The Settings screen appears.
2. Scroll down and touch **Phone**. The Phone Settings screen appears.
3. Touch **Respond with Text**. The Respond with Text screen appears, as shown in **Figure 7**.

4. Touch one of the messages under 'CAN'T TALK RIGHT NOW..." to edit it.
5. Touch **Phone** in the upper left-hand corner. The new preset text messages are saved.

Figure 7: Respond with Text Screen

Adjusting Text Message Settings

Table of Contents

1. Turning iMessage On or Off

The iMessage feature allows you to send free text messages to another iPhone, iPad, or iPod Touch. Turn on iMessage to send a message to another iPhone or to an iPad or iPod touch using the email address assigned to the recipient's iMessage account. By default, iMessage is turned on. When iMessage is turned off and you send a text message to another device, standard text messaging rates apply as set forth by your network provider. To turn iMessage on or off:

1. Touch the ⚙ icon. The Settings screen appears, as shown in **Figure 1**.
2. Scroll down and touch **Messages**. The Message Settings screen appears, as shown in **Figure 2**.
3. Touch the ⬭ switch next to 'iMessage'. The ⬤ switch appears and iMessage is turned on.
4. Touch the ⬤ switch next to 'iMessage'. The ⬭ switch appears and iMessage is turned off.

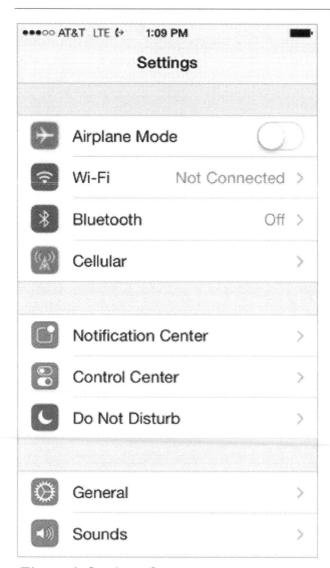

Figure 1: Settings Screen

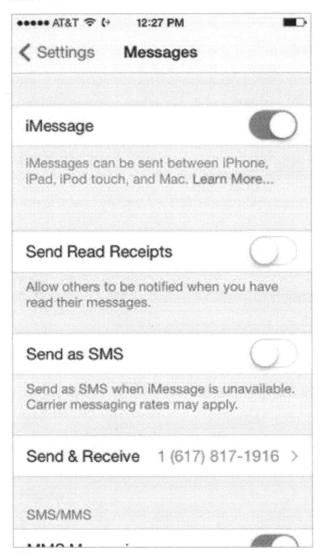

Figure 2: Message Settings Screen

2. Turning Read Receipts On or Off in iMessage

After receiving and opening a message from an iPhone, iPad, or iPod Touch, your iPhone can notify the sender that you have opened and read the message. These notifications are called Read Receipts, and appear under the original message on the sender's screen as "Read", followed by a time. Read Receipts are only compatible with the three Apple devices listed above. To turn Read Receipts on or off:

1. Touch the ![icon] icon. The Settings screen appears.
2. Scroll down and touch **Messages**. The Message Settings screen appears.

3. Touch the ⬤ switch next to 'Send Read Receipts'. The ⬤ switch appears and Read Receipts are turned on.

4. Touch the ⬤ switch next to 'Send Read Receipts'. The ⬤ switch appears and Read Receipts are turned off.

3. Turning 'Send as SMS' On or Off

When a message cannot be sent via iMessage, the iPhone can attempt to send it as a regular text message, or SMS. To turn Send as SMS on or off:

1. Touch the ⬤ icon. The Settings screen appears.
2. Scroll down and touch **Messages**. The Message Settings screen appears.

3. Touch the ⬤ switch next to 'Send as SMS'. The ⬤ switch appears and 'Send as SMS' is turned on.

4. Touch the ⬤ switch next to 'Send as SMS'. The ⬤ switch appears and 'Send as SMS' is turned off.

Note: When 'Send as SMS' is turned off, you will only be able to send a message to an iPhone, iPad, or iPod, which has iMessage enabled.

4. Turning MMS Messaging On or Off

When you are running low on data, it can be useful to disable MMS messaging to avoid receiving unwanted picture messages that will use up the data too quickly. To turn MMS messaging on or off:

1. Touch the ⬤ icon. The Settings screen appears.
2. Scroll down and touch **Messages**. The Message Settings screen appears.

3. Touch the ⬤ switch next to 'MMS Messaging'. The ⬤ switch appears and MMS Messaging is turned off.

4. Touch the ⬤ switch next to 'MMS Messaging'. The ⬤ switch appears and MMS Messaging is turned on.

5. Turning the Subject Field On or Off

The iPhone can attach a subject to each text message it sends when the subject field is enabled. On most phones, the subject will appear in parentheses preceding the message content. To turn the subject field on or off:

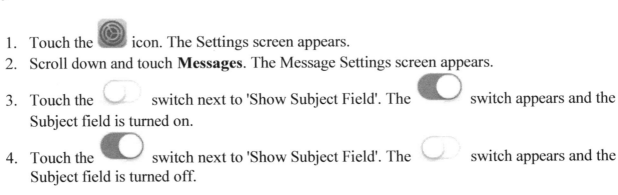

1. Touch the ⊚ icon. The Settings screen appears.
2. Scroll down and touch **Messages**. The Message Settings screen appears.

3. Touch the ⬭ switch next to 'Show Subject Field'. The ⬤ switch appears and the Subject field is turned on.

4. Touch the ⬤ switch next to 'Show Subject Field'. The ⬭ switch appears and the Subject field is turned off.

6. Turning the Character Count On or Off

The Messaging application can show you the number of characters that you have typed when entering a message. To turn the character count on or off:

1. Touch the ⊚ icon. The Settings screen appears.
2. Scroll down and touch **Messages**. The Message Settings screen appears.

3. Touch the ⬭ switch next to 'Character Count'. The ⬤ switch appears and the Character Count is turned on.

4. Touch the ⬤ switch next to 'Character Count'. The ⬭ switch appears and the Character Count is turned off.

7. Turning Group Messaging On or Off

When sending a text message, you can include multiple recipients at the same time. This feature is known as Group Messaging. To turn Group Messaging on or off:

1. Touch the [icon] icon. The Settings screen appears.
2. Scroll down and touch **Messages**. The Message Settings screen appears.

3. Touch the [switch] switch next to 'Group Messaging'. The [switch] switch appears and the Group Messaging is turned on.

4. Touch the [switch] switch next to 'Group Messaging'. The [switch] switch appears and the Group Messaging is turned off.

Adjusting Music Application Settings

Table of Contents

1. Turning 'Shake to Shuffle' On or Off

When the 'Shake to Shuffle' feature is enabled, the iPhone can shuffle the songs it is currently playing when you shake the phone. To turn 'Shake to Shuffle' on or off:

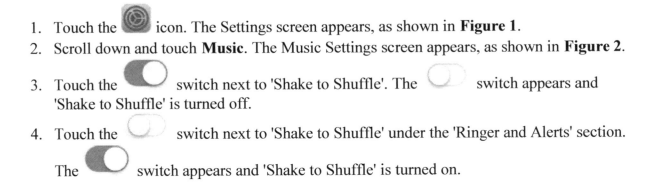

1. Touch the ⊕ icon. The Settings screen appears, as shown in **Figure 1**.
2. Scroll down and touch **Music**. The Music Settings screen appears, as shown in **Figure 2**.
3. Touch the ⬤ switch next to 'Shake to Shuffle'. The ◯ switch appears and 'Shake to Shuffle' is turned off.
4. Touch the ◯ switch next to 'Shake to Shuffle' under the 'Ringer and Alerts' section.

   The ⬤ switch appears and 'Shake to Shuffle' is turned on.

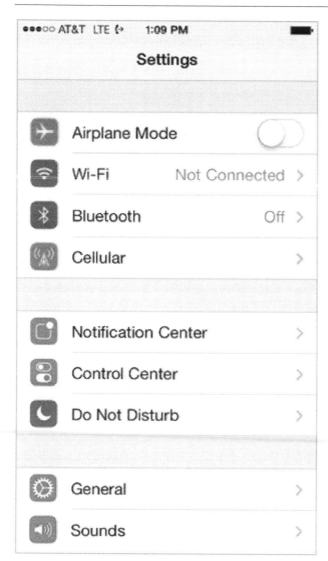

Figure 1: Settings Screen

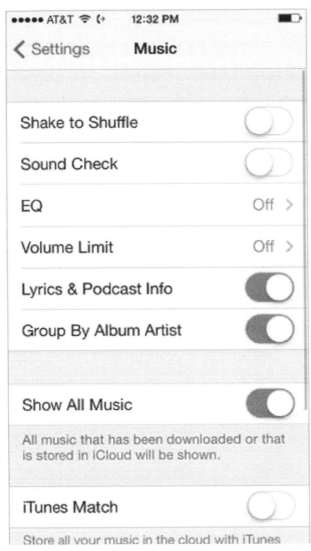

Figure 2: Music Settings Screen

2. Selecting a Pre-Loaded Equalization Setting

The iPhone has several custom, pre-loaded Equalization settings that can be applied in order to improve the sound of your music. To select an Equalization setting:
Note: In order to quickly select the optimal EQ setting for you, turn on some music before performing the steps below. Refer to "Using the Music Application" on page 146 to learn how.

1. Touch the 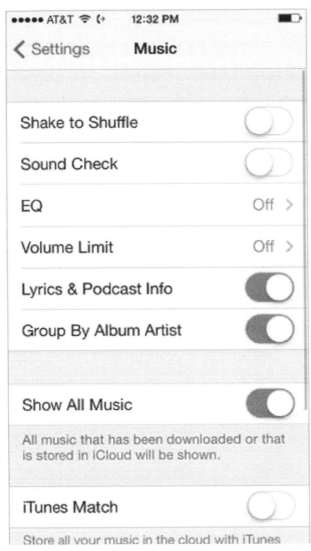 icon. The Settings screen appears.
2. Scroll down and touch **Music**. The Music Settings screen appears.

3. Touch **EQ**. A list of EQ settings appears, as shown in **Figure 3**.
4. Touch an EQ setting. The EQ setting is applied to all music that plays via the Music application.
5. Touch **Music** in the upper left-hand corner of the screen. The EQ setting is saved.

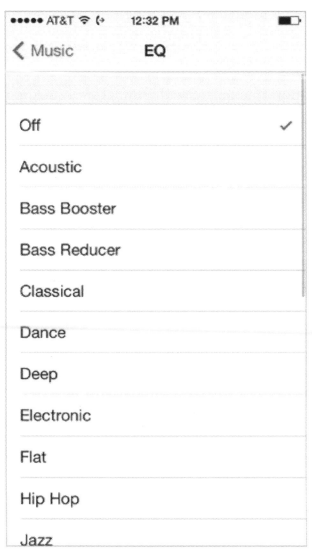

Figure 3: List of EQ Settings

3. Setting a Volume Limit

In order to prevent increasing the volume in the Music application by accidentally pressing the volume buttons, try setting a Volume Limit. To set a Volume Limit:

1. Touch the ⊚ icon. The Settings screen appears.
2. Scroll down and touch **Music**. The Music Settings screen appears.
3. Touch **Volume Limit**. The Volume Limit screen appears, as shown in **Figure 4**.
4. Touch the ⬤ on the ▬▬▬▬▬○ bar and drag it to the desired location. The new volume limit is selected.
5. Touch **Music** in the upper left-hand corner of the screen. The Volume Limit is saved.

Figure 4: Volume Limit Screen

4. Turning Lyrics and Podcast Info On or Off

The iPhone can automatically display the lyrics of a song or the details of a podcast while one of these is playing in the Music application. To turn 'Lyrics and Podcast Info' on or off:

1. Touch the ![icon] icon. The Settings screen appears.
2. Scroll down and touch **Music**. The Music Settings screen appears.
3. Touch the ![switch] switch next to 'Lyrics & Podcast Info'. The ![switch] switch appears and Lyrics and Podcast Info is turned on.

4. Touch the switch next to 'Lyrics & Podcast Info'. The switch appears and Lyrics and Podcast Info is turned off.

5. Choosing which Music Appears in the Music Application

The Music application can either display all of your music, both in the Cloud and on your device, or just the music on your device. To choose which music appears in the music application:

1. Touch the icon. The Settings screen appears.
2. Scroll down and touch **Music**. The Music Settings screen appears.
3. Touch the switch next to 'Show All Music'. The switch appears and both music on your device and in the Cloud will be shown in the Music application.
4. Touch the switch next to 'Show All Music'. The switch appears and only the music on your device will be shown in the Music application.

6. Turning iTunes Match On or Off

iTunes Match is a service that Apple offers at $24.99 per year, which allows you to play songs from Apple's Cloud at the highest quality, as long as the song already exists in your library. iTunes Match songs can be played on any one of your devices. To use iTunes Match, you must first enable it through iTunes on your computer. Click **Store** and then click **Turn On iTunes Match** in iTunes on your computer. You will need to enter your Apple credentials. To turn iTunes Match on or off on the iPhone:

1. Touch the icon. The Settings screen appears.
2. Scroll down and touch **Music**. The Music Settings screen appears.
3. Touch the switch next to 'iTunes Match'. The Password prompt appears.
4. Enter your Apple credentials and touch **OK**. The switch appears and iTunes Match is turned on.
5. Touch the switch next to 'iTunes Match'. The switch appears and iTunes Match is turned off.

Adjusting Photo and Video Settings

Table of Contents

---

1. Turning Photo Stream On or Off

Photo Stream allows you to instantly load photos you have taken on your iPhone to your other registered Apple devices. It accomplishes this by automatically uploading them to the iCloud and then downloading them to the necessary devices. To turn Photo Stream on or off:

1. Touch the ⚙ icon. The Settings screen appears, as shown in **Figure 1**.
2. Scroll down and touch **Photos and Camera**. The Photo Settings screen appears, as shown in **Figure 2**.
3. Touch the ⬭ switch next to 'My Photo Stream'. The ⬬ switch appears and Photo Stream is turned on.
4. Touch the ⬬ switch next to 'My Photo Stream'. The ⬭ switch appears and Photo Stream is turned off.

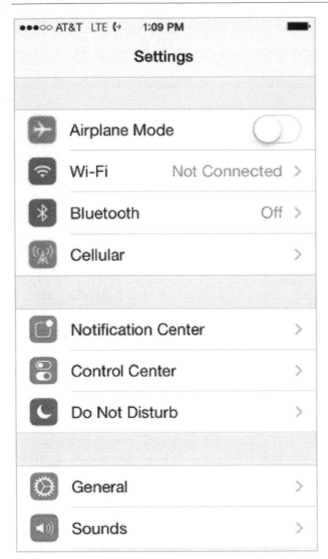

Figure 1: Settings Screen

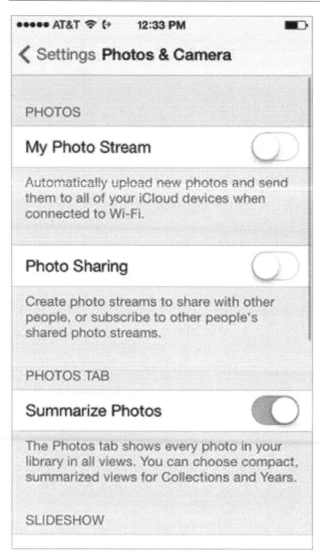

Figure 2: Photo Settings Screen

2. Customizing Slideshow Settings

You can customize the slideshow settings on your iPhone. Refer to *"Starting a Slideshow"* on page 125 to learn how to turn on a slideshow. To customize Slideshow settings:

1. Touch the ⚙ icon. The Settings screen appears.
2. Scroll down and touch **Photos and Camera**. The Photo Settings screen appears.
3. Touch one of the following options or the On/Off switch next to one of the options under the 'Slideshow' section to change the corresponding setting:

- **Play Each Slide For** - Sets the amount of time that each photo remains on the screen during a slideshow.
- **Repeat** - Sets the slideshow to start again from the beginning of the current album after reaching the end.
- **Shuffle** - Sets the photos to appear in random order during a slideshow.

Note: Turning both 'Repeat' and 'Shuffle' on at the same time plays your photos continuously and in random order.

3. Customizing High Dynamic Range (HDR) Camera Settings

When taking photos with the iPhone, you can enable HDR, which will improve picture quality by taking several photos in order to represent actual lighting much more accurately than in a photo taken by a non-HDR camera. To turn on HDR, touch **HDR Off** at the top of the screen while the camera is running. When HDR is turned on, a non-HDR copy of each photo is stored by default. To customize HDR settings:

1. Touch the ⚙ icon. The Settings screen appears.
2. Scroll down and touch **Photos and Camera**. The Photo Settings screen appears.
3. Touch the ⬤ switch next to 'Keep Normal Photo'. The ⬤ switch appears and the iPhone will now delete non-HDR photos while keeping the HDR copy.
4. Touch the ⬤ switch next to 'Keep Normal Photo'. The ⬤ switch appears and the iPhone will keep the non-HDR photo in addition to the HDR copy when taking photos.

Note: An HDR photo takes up more memory on your device than a non-HDR one.

4. Customizing Video Playback Settings

After a video is stopped (not paused), the iPhone can resume playing it from the beginning or from where you last left off. To customize Video Playback settings:

1. Touch the ⚙ icon. The Settings screen appears.
2. Scroll down and touch **Videos**. The Video Settings screen appears, as shown in **Figure 3**.
3. Touch **Start Playing**. The Start Playing screen appears, as shown in **Figure 4**.
4. Touch **From Beginning**. Videos will now resume from the beginning.
5. Touch **Where Left Off**. Videos will now resume where they last left off.

6. Touch **Videos** in the upper left-hand corner of the screen. Your video playback selection is saved.

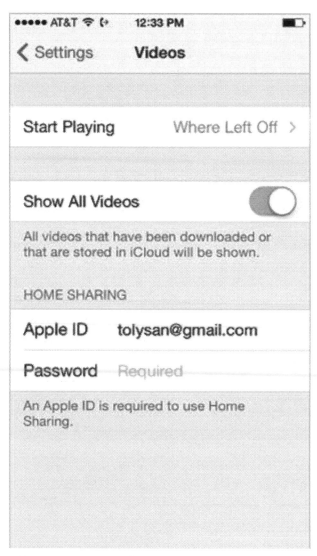

Figure 3: Video Settings Screen

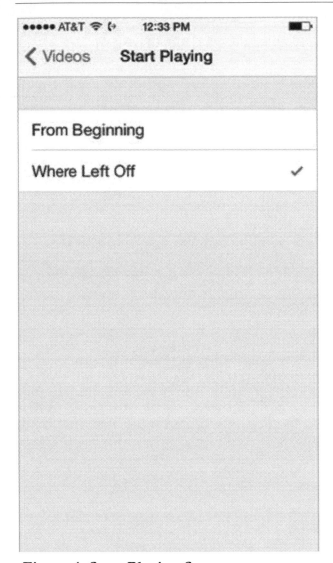

Figure 4: Start Playing Screen

5. Choosing which Videos Appear in the Videos Application

The Music application can either display all of your videos, both in the Cloud and on your device, or just the videos on your device. To choose which music appears in the music application:

1. Touch the ⊚ icon. The Settings screen appears.
2. Scroll down and touch **Videos**. The Video Settings screen appears.

3. Touch the ⬭ switch next to 'Show All Videos'. The ⬬ switch appears and all videos, both on your device and in the Cloud will appear in the Videos application.

4. Touch the ⬬ switch next to 'Show All Videos'. The ⬭ switch appears and only videos on your device will appear in the Videos application.

Tips and Tricks

Table of Contents

1. Maximizing Battery Life

There are several things you can do to increase the battery life of the iPhone:

- Turn off the iPhone while it is charging. To do this, plug the iPhone in and then turn it off.
- Lock the iPhone whenever you are not using it. To lock the iPhone, press the **Sleep/Wake** button at the top of the phone. Refer to *"Button Layout"* on page 9 for the location of the Sleep/Wake button.
- Keep the Auto-lock feature on and set it to a small amount of time to wait before locking the phone when it is idle. Refer to *"Changing Auto-Lock Settings"* on page 240 to learn how to change Auto-lock settings.
- Turn down the brightness and turn off Auto-Brightness. Refer to *"Adjusting the Brightness"* on page 244 to learn how.
- Turn on Airplane mode in areas where there is little or no signal, as the iPhone will continually try to search for service. Refer to *"Turning Airplane Mode On or Off"* on page 209 to learn how to turn on Airplane Mode.
- Make sure to let the battery drain completely and then charge it fully at least once a month. This will help both short-term and long-term battery life.
- Turn off 4G when it is not in use. Refer to *"Turning 4G On or Off"* on page 213 to learn how.
- Turn off Wi-Fi when it is not in use. Refer to *"Using Wi-Fi"* on page 24 to learn how.
- Turn off Location Services when they are not in use. Refer to *"Turning Location Services On or Off"* on page 210 to learn how.

2. Taking a Screenshot

To capture what is on the screen and save it as a photo, press and hold the **Home** button and then press the **Sleep/Wake** Button. Release the buttons and the screen will momentarily flash white. The screenshot is saved to the Camera Roll album.

3. Scrolling to the Top of a Screen

Touch anywhere in the bar at the very top of the screen to quickly scroll to the top of a list, website, etc. The bar is where the signal bars and battery meter are located.

4. Saving an Image While Browsing the Internet

To save an image from Safari to the iPhone, touch and hold the picture until the Image menu appears. Touch **Save Image**. The image is saved to the Camera Roll album.

5. Inserting a Period

When typing a sentence, touch the space bar twice quickly to insert a period and a space at the end of it.

6. Adding an Extension to a Contact's Number

When entering a number for a stored contact, you can add an extension that will be dialed following a short pause after the call is connected. While entering a number, touch the ＋ ＊ ＃ button in the lower left-hand corner of the screen and then touch **Pause**. A comma appears and you can now type an extension. Each comma represents one second that the phone will wait.

7. Navigating the Home Screens

Typically, you get to another Home screen by touching the screen and sliding your finger to the left or right. Alternatively, touch one of the gray dots at the bottom of a Home screen to go to the corresponding one.

8. Typing Alternate Characters

When typing a sentence, insert other characters, such as Á or Ñ, by touching and holding the base letter. A menu of characters appears above the letter. Touch a character to insert it.

9. Deleting Recently Typed Text

This feature is quite a secret. If you have just typed several lines of text and do not want any of it, just give the phone a good shake. A menu appears asking whether to undo the typing.
Touch **Undo**. The typed text is erased. Give the phone another shake to redo the typing. This works in any application or while text messaging.

10. Resetting the iPhone

If the iPhone or an application freezes up or is acting strangely, you may wish to reset the iPhone. This will NOT wipe any data, but simply restart the operating system. To reset the iPhone, hold the **Home** button and **Sleep/Wake** button together until the phone completely shuts off. Continue to hold the buttons until the logo appears. The phone resets and starts up.

11. Viewing the Full Horizontal Keyboard

The full horizontal keyboard provides much better accuracy than the vertical keyboard. Rotate the phone on either side while typing a text message or entering text in another application that supports it to turn on the horizontal keyboard.

12. Calling a Phone Number on a Website

You can call a phone number on a website directly. The number will be blue and underlined, much like a link. Touch the number. The iPhone calls it. If the number is on a website, the iPhone will ask whether to call the number. Touch **Call**. This may not work with all websites.

14. Taking Notes

A convenient way to take notes is by using the built-in Notes application and emailing the notes to yourself. To take notes, touch the ![icon] icon. Touch the ![+] button at the top right of the screen to add a note. Touch the ![share] icon at the bottom of the screen and then touch **Email** to email the note.

15. Recovering Signal After Being in an Area with No Service

Sometimes the iPhone has trouble finding signal after returning from an area where AT&T or Verizon was not available. This issue can sometimes be fixed by turning Airplane Mode on and then back off. Refer to *"Turning Airplane Mode On or Off"* on page 209 to learn how.

16. Changing the Number of Rings Before the iPhone Goes to Voicemail

There is a hidden way to change the number of times the iPhone rings before going to Voicemail. The maximum number of seconds the phone can ring is 30. Have a pen and paper ready, as you will need to enter a long number. To change the number of times the iPhone rings before going to Voicemail:

1. Touch the ![phone] icon and then touch the ![keypad] icon. The Keypad appears.
2. Dial ***#61#** exactly as it appears here and touch **CALL**. When the call is completed, the Voicemail Configuration screen appears.
3. Write down the number that follows "Forwards to." Skip the '+' since you will be typing it in later anyway.
4. Touch **Dismiss**. The call is ended.
5. Dial ***61*+1XXXXXXXXXX*11*tt#** exactly as it appears here, where the X's represent the number you just wrote down and "tt" is the number of seconds you want for the iPhone to ring before going to Voicemail. For example, if the number you wrote down is 1234567890 and the number of seconds you prefer is 30, you would dial *61*+11234567890*11*30#. To make the plus sign appear when dialing a phone number, touch and hold **0**.

6. Touch **CALL.** The number of seconds the iPhone rings is changed and a confirmation appears.
7. Touch **Dismiss**. The call is ended.

Note: To change the ring time back, just repeat these steps. The number you wrote down in step three does not change, so you can proceed to step four if you know it. The default ring time for the iPhone is 20 seconds.

17. Changing the Navigation Icons in the iPod Application

You can change the arrangement of the Navigation icons in the iPod application. While using the iPod Application, touch the icon. The More screen appears. Touch **Edit** at the top right of the screen and then touch any icon on the page and drag it to the bottom of the screen. Release it over another icon. The icons are swapped.

18. Returning to the Last Screen in the Music Application

While listening to music, swipe the screen to the right instead of pressing the Back button to return to the last screen (songs, artists, etc.)

19. Deleting a Song in the Music Application

To delete a song from your iPhone, touch the song and swipe your finger to the left. **DELETE** appears. Touch **DELETE**. The song is deleted.

20. Taking a Picture from the Lock Screen

To take a picture without unlocking the phone, touch the icon in the lower right-hand corner of the screen and slide your finger up. The camera turns on. Press the **Volume Up** button. The camera takes a picture.

21. Assigning a Custom Ringtone to a Contact

You can assign a custom ringtone to any contact in the Phonebook. To assign a ringtone to a contact:

1. Touch the ![icon] icon. The Phonebook appears.
2. Find and touch the contact to which you wish to assign a custom ringtone. The Contact Info screen appears. Refer to *"Finding a Contact"* on page 52 to learn how.
3. Touch **Edit** in the upper right-hand corner of the screen. The Contact Editing screen appears.
4. Touch **Ringtone**. A list of available ringtones appears.
5. Touch a ringtone. The ringtone plays.
6. Touch **Done** in the upper right-hand corner of the screen. The ringtone is selected and the Contact Editing screen appears.
7. Touch **Done** in the upper right-hand corner of the screen. The ringtone is assigned to the contact.

Note: Refer to "Buying Tones in iTunes" on page 138 to learn how to purchase additional ringtones.

22. Opening the Photos Application without Closing the Camera

To open the Photos application while the camera is turned on, touch the photo thumbnail in the bottom left-hand corner of the screen.

23. Inserting Emoticons

The Emoji keyboard contains over 460 new emoticons that can be used when entering text. To learn how to add the Emoji keyboard, refer to *"Adding an International Keyboard"* on page

228 and touch **Emoji** in step 6. After adding the Emoji keyboard, touch the ![globe key] key at the bottom of the virtual keyboard to switch to the Emoji keyboard while typing. The Emoji keyboard appears.

24. Hiding the Keyboard in the Messages Application

While reading a text message, you can hide the keyboard to view more of the conversation at once. Touch the last visible message in the conversation and slide your finger down to the keyboard. The keyboard is hidden.

25. Controlling Web Surfing Using Gestures

Instead of touching the 〈 and 〉 buttons to go back and forward, respectively, you can touch the screen and slide your finger the left or right, respectively.

26. Navigating the Menus Using Gestures

Instead of touching the text in the upper left-hand corner of the screen to return to the previous menu, just touch the left-hand side of the screen and slide your finger to the right.

27. Pausing an Application Download

If you are downloading more than one application at a time, you may wish to pause one of the downloads so that one of the other applications downloads first. To pause an application download, touch the application icon of the application that you wish to pause. Touch the icon again to resume the download.

28. Making a Quick Note for a Contact

You may take a quick note for a contact without having to edit the entire contents of the contact. To make a quick note for a contact, touch **Notes** under 'Facetime' on the contact's information screen. Touch **All Contacts** in the upper left-hand corner of the screen to save the note.

Troubleshooting

Table of Contents

1. iPhone does not turn on

If the iPhone does not power on, try one or more of the following tips:

- **Recharge the iPhone** - Use the included wall charger to charge the battery. If the battery power is extremely low, the screen will not turn on for several minutes. Do NOT use the USB port on your computer to charge the iPhone.
- **Replace the battery** - If you purchased the iPhone a long time ago and have charged and discharged the battery 300-400 times, you may need to replace it. In this case, however, the iPhone may still turn on, but the battery will die much faster than it would in a newer iPhone. Contact Apple to learn how to replace your battery.
- **Reset the iPhone** – This method will not erase any data. Hold down the **Home** button and **Sleep/Wake** button at the same time for 10 seconds. Keep holding the two buttons until the logo appears and the phone restarts.

2. iPhone is not responding

If the iPhone is frozen or is not responding, try one or more of the following. These steps solve most problems on the iPhone.

- **Exit the Application** - If the phone freezes while running an application, hold the **Home** Button for six seconds. The application quits and the iPhone returns to the Home screen.
- **Turn the iPhone Off and then Back On** - If the iPhone is still frozen, try pressing the **Sleep/Wake** button to turn the iPhone off. Keep holding the Sleep/Wake Button until "Slide to Power Off" appears. Slide your finger from left to right over the text. The iPhone turns off. After the screen is completely black, press the **Sleep/Wake** button again to turn the phone back on.
- **Restart the iPhone** - Hold the **Home** button and **Sleep/Wake** button at the same time for 10 seconds or until the logo appears.
- **Remove Media** - Some downloaded applications or music may freeze up the iPhone. Try deleting some of the media that may be problematic after restarting the phone. Refer to *"Deleting an Application"* on page 197 to learn how to delete an application. You may also erase all data at once by doing the following:

Warning: Once erased, data cannot be recovered. Make sure you back up any files you wish to keep.

1. Touch the icon. The Settings screen appears.
2. Touch **General**. The General Settings screen appears.
3. Touch **Reset**. The Reset screen appears.
4. Touch **Erase All Content and Settings**. A confirmation appears.

3. Can't make a call

If the iPhone cannot make outgoing calls, try one of the following:

- If "No Service" is shown at the top left of the screen, the network does not cover you in your location. Try moving to a different location, or even to a different part of a building. Try walking around to find a better signal.
- Turn off Airplane Mode if you have it turned on. If that does not work, try turning Airplane Mode on for 15 seconds and then turning it off. Refer to *"Turning Airplane Mode On or Off"* on page 209 to learn how.
- Make sure you dialed 1 and an area code with the phone number.
- Turn the iPhone off and back on.

4. Can't surf the web

If you have no internet access, there may be little or no service in your area. Try moving to a different location or turning on Wi-Fi. To learn how to turn on Wi-Fi, refer to *"Using Wi-Fi"* on page 29. If you still can't get online, refer to *"iPhone is not responding"* on page 297 for further assistance.

5. Screen or keyboard does not rotate

If the screen does not rotate or the full, horizontal keyboard is not showing when you rotate the phone, it may be one of these issues:

- The application does not support the horizontal view.
- The iPhone is lying flat. Hold the iPhone upright to change the view in applications that support it.
- The rotation lock is on. Press the **Home** button twice quickly and scroll all the way to the left to check. Touch the icon. Screen rotation is unlocked.

6. iTunes does not detect iPhone

If iTunes does not detect the iPhone when connecting it to your computer, try using a different USB port. If that does not work, turn the iPhone off and on again while it is plugged in to the computer. If the iPhone indicates that it is connected, the problem might be with your computer. Try restarting your computer or reinstalling iTunes. Otherwise, refer to *"iPhone is not responding"* on page 303 for assistance.

7. iPhone does not ring or play music, can't hear while talking, can't listen to voicemails

Make sure the volume is turned up. Refer to *"Button Layout"* on page 9 to find the Volume Controls. Check whether you can still hear sound through headphones. The headphone jack is located on the top of the iPhone. If you can hear sound through headphones, try inserting the headphones and taking them out several times. Sometimes the sensor in the headphone jack malfunctions.

8. Low Microphone Volume, Caller can't hear you

If you are talking to someone who can't hear you, try the following:

- Take off any cases or other accessories as these may cover up the microphone.
- When you first take the iPhone out of the box, it comes with a piece of plastic covering the microphone. Make sure to take this plastic off before using the iPhone.
- If the caller cannot hear you at all, you may have accidentally muted the conversation. Refer to *"Using the Mute Function During a Voice Call"* on page 45 to learn how turn Mute on or off.

10. Camera does not work

If the iPhone camera is not functioning correctly, try one of the following:

- Clean the camera lens with a polishing cloth.

- Take off any cases or accessories that may interfere with the camera lens on the back of the iPhone.
- Hold the phone steady when taking a picture. A shaky hand often results in a blurry picture.
- Try leaning against a stationary object to stabilize your hand.
- If you cannot find the icon on your Home screen, try the following:

    1. Touch the icon. The Settings screen appears.
    2. Touch **General**. The General Settings screen appears.
    3. Touch **Restrictions**. The Restrictions screen appears.
    4. Touch **Disable Restrictions**. All restrictions are disabled.

11. iPhone shows the White Screen of Death

If the iPhone screen has gone completely white, try restarting or restoring the phone. Refer to *"iPhone is not responding"* on page 297 to learn how.

12. "iPhone needs to cool down" message appears

If you leave the iPhone in your car on a hot day or expose it to direct sunlight for too long, one of the following may happen:

- Device stops charging
- Weak signal
- Screen dims
- iPhone breaks completely
- "iPhone needs to cool down" message appears

Before using the iPhone, allow it to cool. The iPhone works best in temperatures between 32°F and 95°F (0°C to 35°C). While it is turned off, store the iPhone at temperatures between -4°F and 113°F (-20°C to 45°C).

13. Display does not adjust brightness automatically

If the iPhone does not brighten in bright conditions or does not become dimmer in dark conditions, try taking any cases or accessories off. A case may block the light sensor, located at the top of the phone near the earpiece. Also, check to make sure that Auto-Brightness is turned on. Refer to *"Adjusting the Brightness"* on page 244 to learn how to turn on Auto-Brightness.

Index

21858953R00173

Printed in Great Britain
by Amazon